The Plays and Fiction of
Luigi Pirandello

■■■■■■■■■■■■■■■■■■■■■■■■■■■■■■■■■■■■■

Selected Essays by
Anne Paolucci

Copyright © 2009 by Anne Paolucci

Publisher's Cataloguing-in-Publication Data

Paolucci, Anne

    The plays and fiction of Luigi Pirandello : selected essays / by Anne Paolucci.— 1st ed.— Middle Village, NY : Griffon House Pub., c2009.

    p. ; cm.
    ISBN: 978-1-932107-27-2
    Includes bibiographical references.

    1. Pirandello, Luigi, 1867-1936—Criticism and interpretation. I. Title.

PQ4835.17 Z7232 2009
852/.912—dc22   0907

Published by
Griffon House Publications
P. O. Box 790095, Middle Village, New York 11379

CONTENTS

Author's Preface v

PART ONE: *BACKGROUND AND REPUTATION*

Introduction to Pirandello's Theater ... 3

Pirandello, "Father of the Contemporary Theater" ... 7

Pirandello and the Waiting Stage of the Absurd (With some Observations on a New "Critical Language") ... 24

Bentley on Pirandello: Forty Years Later ... 32

PART TWO: *CRITICAL ANALYSES*

Research Notes, *Chronicle of Higher Education*, June 12, 1991 (Review of "Sicilian Themes and the Restructured Stage") ... 40

Sicilian Themes and the Restructured Stage: The Dialectic of Fiction and Drama in the Work of Luigi Pirandello ... 41

Narrative in Pirandello's Plays ... 52

The New Humor ... 79

Comedy and Paradox in Pirandello's Plays (An Hegelian Perspective) ... 88

Dramatic Argument on Stage ... 107

The Creative Will ... 119

The Psychology of the Alienated: The Women in Pirandello's Plays ... 127

PART THREE: *COMPARATIVE STUDIES*

Pirandello's *Liolà* and Machiavelli's *Mandragola* ... 149

Monolog Drama: Paul Claudel and Luigi Pirandello ... 159

"Improvisation" as "Script": Carlo Goldoni and Luigi Pirandello ... 172

PART FOUR: *THE LARGER VIEW*

Toward a National Theater ... 181

"Pirandello's Introduction to the Italian Theater" (Translated by Anne Paolucci) ... 193

For
ROBERT BRUSTEIN,
who was among the first to grasp
the genial innovations of Pirandello's theater
and to bring them to life on stage

"It seems just yesterday, but it was actually many years ago that a nimble little maid entered the service of my art; and notwithstanding her long years at the job, she is still young and fresh. Her name is Fantasy." LUIGI PIRANDELLO
Preface to *Six Characters in Search of an Author*

". . . the playwrights of The Theater of the Absurd have forever altered our responses to the theater." EDWARD ALBEE

"American Theater is in a state of protracted adolescence . . . it has a provincial air." JOHN GASSNER
The Theater in Our Time (1954)

AUTHOR'S PREFACE

Writing about Pirandello over three decades ago, director-critic Robert Brustein, for many years the Artistic Director of the American Repertory Theater in Cambridge, Massachusetts, stated unequivocally that "Pirandello's influence on the drama of the twentieth century is immeasurable" and hailed the 1934 Nobel Laureate in Literature as the "Father of the Contemporary Theater." He makes his point by listing what all the major European playwrights drew from Pirandello and made their own — an impressive roster, which includes Albert Camus, Jean-Paul Sartre, Eugene O'Neill, Thornton Wilder, Jack Gelber, Harold Pinter, Edward Albee, Eugene Ionesco, Samuel Beckett, Jean Anouilh, Jean Giraudoux, and Jean Genet.

Earlier critics like Eric Bentley and Francis Fergusson had also recognized in Pirandello's plays something unique and exciting; but in spite of their high praise, these three perceptive writers were in a minority. Nor did Broadway take notice. American productions have been few and far-between and those that have been staged over the years have drawn mixed response from our critics and audiences. Long after Europe and the rest of the world had enthusiastically recognized the new stage Pirandello had forged, America still lagged far behind. The playwright who revolutionized the European theater over eight decades ago, who gave the impetus to playwrights throughout the world, is still virtually unknown in the United States.

In the Preface to *Luigi Pirandello: The Recovery of the Modern Stage for Dramatic Art* — a book Harry T. Moore (at the time editor of the Crosscurrents/Modern Critiques series of Southern Illinois University Press) invited me to write back in the early seventies — Moore was perhaps overly optimistic about Pirandello's future in the United States:

... it is good at this time to have this examination of Pirandello, for he is becoming better known as his plays are being oftener produced than before ... and because more people are reading his work. Pirandello ... has become not only a man for this season, but one for future seasons as well.

Published two years after *From Tension to Tonic: The Plays of Edward Albee*, my book on Pirandello recalled and clarified comparisons I'd made between the two playwrights in the earlier study. I traced Pirandello's new theater from the paradoxes of early plays like *Liolà* to the last three "myth" plays, where dramatic action moves into an epic dimension and dramatic dialogue turns into lyric voices. I probed the novelty of the Pirandellian stage — his open-ended resolutions, the dissolution of character into internal, subjective states, his insistence that reality is shaped by inner conviction rather than external objective facts. I argued that Pirandello was not a relativist (as so often professed) but a Socratic critic of "reality," bent on redefining experience as the expression of the *will*. I described how he succeeded in preserving not only the basic values that he seemed to be undermining, but the very illusion of realism on stage. My conclusion was that Pirandello was indeed the father of the contemporary theater and, by extension, also the creator of "Theater of the Absurd."

The book was well received but certainly didn't make the "best-seller" lists. Today, Pirandello remains at best an anomaly among scholars, rarely staged outside college campuses. It comes as no surprise that our own Edward Albee, the only American playwright inspired by the new European theater forged by Pirandello, should have suffered a similar fate: we have not advanced much since John Gassner's harsh judgment. The Realism introduced into our drama by Eugene O'Neill in the first decades of the 20th century, that reached its peak with Arthur Miller in the 40s and 50s, continues to dominates our stage — though stale and repetitive at this point in time — leaving no room in our "legitimate" theater for much else.

When the suggestion was made that I bring together my scattered essays in a single volume, I saw an opportunity to give Pirandello's works fresh visibility.

The book is in four sections: general and background topics; specific analyses of the plays; comparative studies; and, finally, larger issues and Pirandello's insightful essay of the history of the Italian theater.

Rereading these essays at a distance in time, I found some revision inevitable. I avoided consolidation, however, firmly convinced that rephrasing arguments from different perspectives reinforces important ideas.

ANNE PAOLUCCI
New York, March 2009

PART ONE
BACKGROUND AND REPUTATION

The New York Times

Sunday, March 27, 1994

The City

Section **13**

Test Your Literary I.Q.: Level 1

Each of these writers is the hero, or heroine, of a literary society in New York. Read the clues and guess who they are.

By CONSTANCE L. HAYS

RONALD WEITZ spends his days in Brooklyn, overseeing a squad of city social workers who try to find help for cocaine-addicted babies.

But every few weeks he takes up a well-worn paperback, tones up his self-taught brogue and joins two dozen other New Yorkers to plumb the richly double-entendre'd depths of "Finnegans Wake." They read, reread and try to filter meaning from a few pages at a time. Three years beyond "Riverrun," they are still only 447 pages deep.

Ask Mr. Weitz to explain the fascination, and he settles for the simplest possible terms. "Joyce," he says, "has always appealed to me, for some reason or another."

Call it weird or escapist or write it off to the usual urban quest for identity. But across New York, literary societies are flourishing, focused on everything from children's books to murder mysteries to the fusty niceties of Victorian England. There is a group for fans of Anthony Trollope and another devoted to Mark Twain, one for Luigi Pirandello, another dedicated to C. S. Lewis, and several that study the "canon" of Sherlock Holmes.

Associated Press, 1930

1. Elementary

Culver Pictures

6. A woman of sensibility

2. Ghostwriter

Berenice Abbott

7. "Stephen Hero"

Your Literary I.Q.: Level 2

Pioneer Press, 1928

4. The feminist muse of Mankato, Minn.

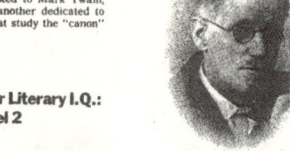

5. How They Lived Then

Feeling smug?
For Level 2,
Read on.

Bruni Foto Agenzia, 1930

3. One playwright in search of an I.D.

8. Archie Goodwin's Samuel Johnson

Still feeling smug?
Answers! ⟶

INTRODUCTION TO PIRANDELLO'S THEATER

A master of short stories, novels, and plays, the Sicilian-born 1934 Nobel Laureate in Literature, Luigi Pirandello, is perhaps best known for *Six Characters in Search of an Author* — the play that revolutionized the European theater in 1923 and launched his career internationally. It is Pirandello's most popular full-length play, a frequent offering of campus and community theaters. A close second is his one-act play, *The Man With the Flower in His Mouth*.

Commercial productions on the American stage, however, have been few and far between. Translations are either old or not up to par; and until recently, new ones (as well as commercial productions) had to have the approval of the Pirandello heirs — a condition introduced years ago by Toby Cole, for decades the agent in charge of Pirandello's dramatic works in America. Cole insisted that any staging of Pirandello had to be a "star production" with an "all-star cast," etc. Her mistakenly protective restrictions kept Pirandello at a distance, with the result that many of his plays still wait to be discovered here in the United States. A welcome exception is the translation in one volume, by William Murray, of Pirandello's eleven one-act plays.[1] These include, in addition to *The Man With the Flower in His Mouth*, such gems as *At the Exit* (about half-baked ghosts waiting for their last wish to be fulfilled in order to move into oblivion) — the inspiration, some scholars and critics say, for Thornton Wilder's *Our Town*.

Pirandello's novelty was not in the "gimmicks" Eugene O'Neill made good use of — masks, shrinking rooms, etc. — but stemmed from a totally new vision of the stage, clearing it of the outworn conventions of the realistic theater first introduced among us by O'Neill and given a solid impetus well into the twentieth century by Arthur Miller. O'Neill can easily be imitated because his novelties can be abstracted and applied to other contexts. Pirandello's innovations stem from an organic restructuring of the stage itself. He is, according to director-critic Robert Brustein, "the most seminal dramatist of our time," from whom the major playwrights of our post World War age have drawn their own inspiration.

In his agony over the nature of existence, he anticipates Sartre and Camus. In his insights into the disintegration of personality and the isolation of man, he anticipates Samuel Beckett. In his unremitting war on language, theory, concepts and the collective mind, he anticipates Eugene Ionesco. In his approach to the concept of truth and illusion he anticipates Eugene O'Neill and later Harold Pinter and Edward Albee. In his experiments with the theater, he anticipates a host of experimental dramatists including Thonton Wilder and Jack Gelber. And in his concept of man as a role-playing animal, he anticipates Jean Genet.[2]

Pirandello uses his restructured stage to dramatize the dissolution of the "givens" we all tend to accept in life. and starts us thinking about who we really are. We think we are one person, we accept certain people with certain names as our parents: of course we know who we are, right? Pirandello forces us to examine the "truths" we take for granted. The mirrored images that come back to us from the people around us, from events we have witnessed or have taken part in, are not external objective facts for us to pick up and store away. Nothing can be assumed in trying to capture the true self.

We wear many masks, Pirandello tells us; every day, every hour, every minute we are different people. We have our public faces and our private ones. He makes his own the Socratic adage, "Know thyself." He does this by undermining so-called "facts," as in *Right You Are (If You Think So!)*, where Laudisi plays the Socratic cynic and forces everyone to probe what appear to be obvious "facts." Brustein singles out this insistence on restructuring the world around us to conform with our inner mandates as Pirandello's "most original achievement . . . the dramatization of the very act of creation."³

The intense Sicilian core is strong in all of Pirandello's writings. Some see it as too narrow a perspective perhaps; if so, we can always substitute for it something that is closer to our own experience. The point to remember, however, as T. S. Eliot tells us (always the reliable arbiter in literary matters), is that the "two characteristics that must be found together, in any author whom I should single out as one of the landmarks of a national literature [are] strong local flavour and unconscious universality."⁴ Sicilian life is what Pirandello knows first hand. It is at the center of most of his plays, even the "theater plays," which won immediate international acclaim.

Pirandello's new stage forces the audience to become a "player," no longer passive, waiting simply to be entertained. He does this by breaking down the barriers between the stage and the audience, especially in the "theater plays," where action is interrupted, actors and directors address the audience, actors move in and out of their roles, etc. These plays are also open-ended, which means they do not proceed to a conventional resolution but conclude abruptly, unexpectedly, the action aborted in the middle of things.

The "theater plays" offer the best examples of Pirandello's innovative genius because the theater lends itself beautifully as a venue for the stage of life. It's a whole new vision: theater as life, theater as the mirrored image of self. The actors in their layered roles reach out to the audience and draw us surreptitiously into the action.

This is an existential stage, anticipated by Pirandello in the early part of the century, and given the fullest expression by post-World War II playwrights, particularly in France. It calls for "subjective correlatives" rather than social or political or religious reform. It is not the realistic theater of greater social awareness, of political commentary. It is a theater that forces *inwardness*, self-awareness, the dialectic of consciousness and self-consciousness, as we search for our true selves. It is a theater that depicts what Albert Camus defines as the isolation of man, "the divorce of man from his environment."[5]

Pirandello anticipated this pervasive mandate and created the dramatic idiom for it. His new theater leads us to an awareness that we must build for ourselves the road on which we walk, lay down each brick, each stone along the way, every day of our lives. There are no external directional signals; certainty lies in ourselves, in our self-conscious recognition of the life around us, a world that must be scrutinized and evaluated, redefined in our terms, before it can be accepted. It depicts Reality as an act of *will*.

NOTES

1. William Murray, trans., *Pirandello's One-Act Plays* (Samuel French, Inc. New York, 1970).

2. Robert Brustein, *Theater of Revolt*. (See: Anne Paolucci, *Pirandello's Theater: The Recovery of the Modern Stage for Dramatic Art* (Southern Illinois University Press/Feffer & Simons, Carbondale/Edwardsville, London/Amsterdam, 1974; rpt. Griffon House Publications, Smyrna, DE, 2002), pp. 5-6.

3. *Ibid.*, p. 5.

4. T.S. Eliot, "American Literature and the American Language," *To Criticize the Critic* (Farrar, Straus, & Giroux, New York, 1965), p. 54.

5. Albert Camus, *Le Mythe de Sisyphe* (Paris, 1942. Cited by Martin Esslin, *The Theater of the Absurd* (New York, 1961), p. xix.

Pirandello, "Father of the Contemporary Theater"

Six Characters in Search of an Author (1921), the first of Pirandello's well known three "theater plays," was booed off the stage when it premiered in Rome. It was the Paris production of Georges and Ludmilla Pitoëff, in 1923, that made Pirandello (and the Pitoëffs) an overnight sensation. In the years that followed he became known throughout the world, often traveling (especially in later years) to the various countries in Europe, Asia, South America, wherever his plays were being performed. He was a hit everywhere, except in the United States.

He came here, already world-renowned, to promote his plays. Among those who accompanied him was his leading lady, the woman whom he loved desperately but who never returned that love, Marta Abba. There were meetings in Hollywood with directors and producers like Otto Kahn and Irving Thalberg; negotiations with Universal, Metro-Goldwyn-Mayer, Paramount, RKO; telegrams and visits from stars like Marlene Dietrich and Silvia Sydney; contacts with potential stars for film versions of some of his plays; but the only positive outcome of all these efforts was the film version of *Come tu mi vuoi* (*As You Desire Me*), which starred Greta Garbo. It was not the best choice for introducing Pirandello to an American audience, but it was an excellent vehicle for Garbo.[1]

Why has Pirandello failed to attract American audiences? One reason is that after his death all productions as well as translations had to be approved by former agent Toby Cole (later, by the Pirandello heirs). The result has been to stifle all large efforts to promote Pirandello in the United States. The one im-

---

Part of this essay was delivered as a lecture at the Graduate School of The City University of New York, October 29, 1997.

portant production in the last several decades to have gained approval was the 1973 *Enrico IV*, at Lincoln Center, starring Rex Harrison — who was heard to complain, "What the hell is this play all about?"

Restrictions on translations and major productions in the United States have had a deleterious effect: Pirandello cannot gain a large following where his work is virtually inaccessible. What has kept Pirandello from total oblivion are community/regional productions, dramatic readings, special panels and events like those encouraged and sponsored for decades by The Pirandello Society of America at literary meetings, especially the annual and regional conventions of The Modern Language Association of America. As President of the Society for over seventeen years, I made sure that it was represented as an Affiliated Association at those meetings and encouraged dramatic readings, whenever possible, as part of our programs. For over twenty-five years, I personally included Pirandello in all my under-graduate and graduate courses at St. John's University in New York and, when asked to speak or lecture on drama at other universities or to community groups, I made a point of bringing Pirandello into my presentations. But even the limited results of that effort have been eroded, since there are few people academically prepared or willing to take on an author who is, at best, on the fringes of the mainstream here in the United States.

A few important American scholar-critics have recognized Pirandello's importance, but they too have had a limited audience, mostly academics. Eric Bentley wrote, as early as 1946:

> Ostensibly Pirandello's plays and novels are about the relativity of truth, multiple personality, and the different levels of reality. But it is neither these subjects nor — precisely — his treatment of them that constitutes Pirandello's individuality. The themes grow tiresome after a while, and those who find nothing else in Pirandello give him up as a bad job. The novelist Franz

Kafka was long neglected because his work also gave the impression of philosophic obsession and willful eccentricity. Then another and deeper Kafka was discovered.[2]

Bentley singled out the most important feature in plays like *Liolà* (1916) and *Six Characters in Search of an Author* (1921) as "the peculiar relation of intellect to feeling." When most critics were struggling to understand Pirandello's new theater in traditional terms, often dismissing him as "cerebral" or glossing over what they could not grasp, Bentley was well ahead of the game, dismissing the popular but misleading notion of the plays as exercises in relativity, open-ended as regards meaning. That notion should be set aside, he insisted, using the example of *Così è (se vi pare)* (*Right You Are! If You Think So!*) to bring home that message:

> [T]here is actually nothing in the plot of *Right You Are!* to indicate that there can be no correct version of the story. . . . The unusual thing is that we do not know what it is. . . . The truth, Pirandello wants to tell us again and again, is concealed, *concealed*, CONCEALED! It is not his business to uncover the problem and solve it for us. . . . The solution is the problem.[3]

Bentley's notion of the "solution" as the "problem," the "concealment" of a conclusion to be discovered, takes us to the very center of Pirandello's stage.

Another perceptive critic, Francis Fergusson, had this to say in *The Idea of a Theater: The Act of Drama in Changing Perspective* (1949):

> The most fertile property of Pirandello's dramaturgy is his use of the stage itself. By so boldly accepting it for what it is, he freed it from the demand which modern realism has made of it, that it be a literal copy of scenes off stage; and also from the exorbitant Wagnerian demand, that it be an absolutely obedient instrument of hypnosis in the power of the artist. Thus he brought to light once more the wonderful property which the stage does have: of defining the primitive and subtle medium of the dramatic art. "After Pirandello" — to take him

symbolically rather than chronologically — the way was open for Yeats and Lorca, Cocteau and Eliot. The search could start once more for a modern poetry of the theater, and even perhaps for an idea of the theater comparable to that of the Greeks yet tenable in the modern world.[4]

When Jean Paul Sartre in the late fifties was asked to name the most timely and modern dramatist, his answer was: "most certainly Pirandello." And to that same question, Georges Neveux replied:

> Without Pirandello and without the Pitoëffs (because one can no longer separate them, the genius of the Pitoëffs having given its form to Pirandello's) we would have had neither Salacrou, nor Anouilh, nor today Ionesco, nor . . . but I shall stop, this enumeration would be endless. The entire theatre of an era came out of the womb of that play, *Six Characters*.

Later, Ionesco would say: "[L]uigi Pirandello is the manifestation of the inalterable archtype of the idea of the theater we have in us."[5]

But it was director-critic Robert Brustein, who gave the most provocative assessment of Pirandello's new theater, opening up a whole new critical perspective, a crucial one in the ongoing efforts to find a proper and adequate critical language for Pirandello's new stage. Writing about the "Father of the contemporary theater" in "Pirandello's Drama of Revolt," Brustein states unambiguously that the playwright's "most original achievement in his experimental plays [is] the dramatization of the very act of creation," his dramatis personae being the living signatures of his artistry, "both the product and the process." He concludes emphatically that Pirandello is without question "the most *seminal* dramatist of our time . . . his influence on the drama of the twentieth century . . . immeasurable." He goes on to list what every major dramatist took from Pirandello.[6]

What these critics have done is force us to look at the innovative theater of Pirandello as something qualitatively different from what had come before, to recognize it as an open-ended experience rich with possibilities: its players depicted as states of being, levels of awareness; the stage itself under constant transformation even as we watch. Their insightful comments, however, had minimal impact on a general public not prepared to listen. In the United States, Pirandello failed to achieve the solid footing he enjoyed in the rest of the world, where he had managed, with a single play, to overhaul the traditional realistic stage.

Soon after his return from Germany, where he had earned a degree in linguistics at the University of Bonn, he married the daughter of his father's business partner — a marriage that produced three children but had a tragic effect on Pirandello's wife Antonietta, who grew increasingly despondent, eventually became violent, and ultimately had to be committed. They had moved to Rome, where he taught high school and raised his young family. In his spare time he began to write short stories, which found ready readers and a ready market. His first novel, *Il fu Mattia Pascal*, appeared in 1904, that too an immediate success. But it wasn't until more than a decade later, at the age of fifty, that he began to write plays.

It all started when "Il maestro," as Pirandello was often referred to, was asked to write some scripts for the celebrated Sicilian actor, Angelo Musco. His earliest ones, in the language of his native Agrigento (translated by the playwright himself, later, into "official Italian"), were written expressly for Musco. Had Pirandello not responded to that request by the actor's friends, the history of the contemporary theater might have been very different.

A number of one-act plays were produced during this period, all of them set in poverty-stricken Sicilian villages, all of them depicting in a variety of ways the dismantling of illusions. Some, paradoxically, are hilariously funny. A perfect example of humor and compassion softening the harsh criticism of prejudice and hypocritical self-interest is *La patente* (*The*

License). In this short play, a man who has suffered a number of setbacks is shunned by everyone as a carrier of the "evil eye," his family ostracized. In desperation, he sues the town officials and forces a court ruling that he knows will go against him. In fact, he makes sure he will lose, by giving the officials all the evidence they need for *them* to win the case. Understandably, this confuses those who would like to spare the poor man further pain and humiliation. They advise him to drop a case he can't possibly win. He finally explains the clever strategy he has worked out. Once he is officially recognized as the carrier of the "evil eye," he tells them, he will advertise the fact by have calling cards printed with the "official" title with which the court has saddled him. He will distribute his cards to the village shop owners and in that way earn money to feed his family. When the others still appear confused, he goes on to describe how he will place himself every morning in the doorway of this or that shop, where no one will dare to enter while he — the embodiment of back luck — is standing there. The owner, faced with losing his clients, naturally will pay him to move on, and so he does: on to the next shop, and the next and the next. Losing the court battle will insure him the livelihood he and his family need to survive. He has made good use of their hypocrisy and prejudice, casting himself wholeheartedly into the role he is forced to assume, to the point of dressing in a revolting costume of rags.

This is funny, of course, but the laughter it provokes is a nervous uncertain one, just as the unexpected reversal of common sense is actually the most sensible solution possible. The humor in all this lies precisely in the reversals we witness: what appears ludicrous at first turns out to be something quite different. In his treatise on humor, *L'Umorismo*, Pirandello explains how we might laugh at a heavily made-up middle-aged woman trying to appear young and attractive — perhaps for a young lover. She is comical in her excesses. But if we stop to consider why she has assumed that pathetic mask, we might realize that she is trying desperately to hold on to an illusion, to retain something precious. In that awareness, our response will change; the woman may appear pathetic but no longer comical, to be laughed at. She carries the kind of burden we all must assume sooner or later. Her frailties, her excesses, are ours as well.

Pirandello defined this kind of humor as *il sentimento del contrario,* an awareness of the paradox in things. It is the characteristic humor of the Absurd: we find it in Ionesco's *The Bald Soprano* and *The Lesson,* in Beckett's *Waiting for Godot,* in Albee's *The Zoo Story* and *The Man Who Had Three Arms.* It is humor with a vengeance, humor that stops short of painful grimacing. It is a humor that forces us to face our own inadequacies, our own prejudices, our own role-playing. Pirandello explains at one point:

> . . . the comic writer will merely laugh, being content to deflate this metaphor of ourselves created by spontaneous illusion; the satirist will feel disdain towards it; the humorist does neither; through the ridiculousness of the discovery, he will see the serious and painful side; he will disassemble the construction, but not solely to laugh at it; and, instead of feeling disdain, he will rather, in his laughter, feel compassion.[7]

Those who insist on still preening themselves before their public will obviously see such humor as an excess verging on hysteria or madness. And it is no accident that Pirandello's plays (as also his fiction) often carry that message. The "madness" of Enrico IV, like that of Hamlet's, like Jerry's in *The Zoo Story,* like the exchanges between Pozzo and Lucky in *Waiting for Godot,* like the craziness of Mr. and Mrs. Smith in *The Bald Soprano* is obviously not clinical insanity but a paradoxical metaphor. It is indeed an excess, the result of insurmountable odds, of unrelieved frustration and debilitating despair. It stems from the inability to communicate adequately what is inside us, to explain and share one's convictions and certainties. In such a context, laughter is an embarrassed awareness of our limitations. Pirandello describes the painful dialectic from simple consciousness to self-awareness in this carefully structured analysis:

> The oneness of the soul . . . contradicts the historical concept of the human soul. Its life is a changing equilibrium; it is a continual awakening and obliterating of emotions, tendencies, and ideas; an incessant fluctuating between contradictory terms, and an oscillating between such extremes as hope and fear, truth and falsehood, beauty and ugliness, right and wrong, etc. If in the obscure view of the future a bright plan of action suddenly appears or the flower of pleasure is vaguely seen to shine, soon there also appears our memory of the past, often dim and sad, to avenge the rights of experience; or our sulky and unruly sense of the present will intervene to restrain our spirited imagination. This conflict of memories, hopes, forebodings, perceptions, and ideals, can be seen as a struggle of various souls which are all fighting among themselves for the exclusive and final power over our personality. . . . Life is a continual flux which we try to stop, to fix in stable and determined forms, both inside and outside ourselves, because we are already fixed forms, forms which move in the midst of other immobile forms and which however can follow the flow of life until the movement gradually slowing and becoming more and more rigid, eventually ceases. The forms in which we seek to stop, to fix in ourselves this constant flux are the concepts, the ideals with which we would like consistently to comply, all the fictions we create for ourselves, the conditions, the state in which we tend to stabilize ourselves. But within ourselves, in what we call the soul and is the life in us, the flux continues, indistinct under the barriers and beyond the limits we impose as a means to fashion a consciousness and a personality. . . . In certain moments of turmoil all these fictitious forms are hit by the flux and collapse miserably under its thrust; and even what does not flow under the barrier and beyond the limits — that which is distinctly clear to us and which we have carefully channelled into our feelings, into the duties we have

imposed upon ourselves, into the habits we have marked out for ourselves — in certain moments of floodtide, [all of that] overflows and upsets everything.[8]

Even in his late "myth" plays, where he reviews social mandates (*La colonia, The New Colony*), religious faith (*Lazzaro, Lazarus*), and the very nature of art in his last unfinished play (*I giganti della montagna, The Mountain Giants*), Pirandello is faithful to his central subject: the paradoxical life within us, the illusions that must be discarded, the search for clarity. And in that effort, in the early plays as well as the late ones, humor plays an integral part.

Although not yet in the realm of was to become the new European theater of the twentieth century, two early full-length plays, *Pensaci, Giacomino* and *Liolà* — the latter, an intriguing romantic inversion of the Roman story of the rape of Lucrece, which Niccolo Machiavelli had dramatized with bitter irony in his masterpiece, *Mandragola* — already suggest the paradoxes, reversals, and doubts that characterize the later plays. There is nothing tentative about these early plays, as there was nothing tentative about his short stories and novels. They are perfectly realized. With stunning clarity, especially in *Liolà* (1916), Pirandello puts traditions and conventions to a rigorous test that leads to an unexpected conclusion, at the same time avoiding all hint of scandal and any suggestion of undermining the solidly rooted Sicilian values — the core of these and many later plays as well. He used as he had in his fiction, what he knew best: the difficulties of a closed society, its poverty-stricken people, the impossibility for most of the inhabitants of that society to free themselves from their oppressive environment, a life of weary resignation, from birth to death. One of his later novels, *I vecchi e i giovani* (*The Old and the Young*), reminiscent in many ways of Lampadusa's *Il Gattopardo* (*The Leopard*), focuses on the plight of Sicily, after the unification of Italy, when the new national government betrayed the Sicilians, failing to fulfill the promises made to them.

Liolà focuses on the struggle for economic as well as emotional survival in that closed society. Mita, a pretty but poor young village girl, has been forced to marry a cranky and miserly older man, a widower, to insure her future as well as that of her widowed mother. The old man berates her for not producing the heir he needs; but everyone knows that the fault is not with Mita, who is healthy enough to bear dozens of children, but in Zio Simone, who never produced children with his first wife. All along, Mita has been in love with Liolà, a handsome happy-go-lucky young man, poor but hardworking, who lives with his mother, her only means of support. Liolà loves Mita, but he knows there is no future for them and has kept a discreet distance, although he has fathered three bastards with other young women all too ready to lend themselves to him. Honest, in his own way, Liolà has acknowledged the children and brought them into his house, where he and his mother are raising them. But when another village girl, Tuzza, plots with her mother and the old man to provide Zio Simone with the heir he craves, by offering him (in exchange for security and other benefits) her unborn child by Liolà, the young man secretly plots, in return, to insure Mita's future by giving her the heir her husband craves. There is no lust behind this scheme, simply an answer — the only possible answer — to an unacceptable situation that, if ignored, will undermine Mita's position in her own household. Mita, of course, is scandalized by the suggestion, but Liolà argues persuasively and in the end the girl agrees. Their secret will never be revealed; Zio Simone will be able to boast that he is virile and potent; he will have a "legitimate" heir and Tuzza's bastard will no longer be needed. Here, deception means, paradoxically, turning the accepted values upside down in order to right a terrible wrong.

Five years later, in 1921, the first of the three so-called "theater plays" appeared. With *Sei personaggi in cerca d'autore* (*Six Characters in Search of an Author*), Pirandello found the new medium that was to serve as inspiration and model for the theater of the twentieth century.

Here too, nothing was uncertain, tentative. *Six Characters* was followed quickly by two similar, equally extraordinary and ingenious plays, *Ciascuno a suo modo* (1924) (*Each in His Own Way*), and *Questa sera si recita a soggetto* (1928) (*Tonight We Improvise*) — all three dramatizing the experience of a shifting stage.

In the first, a group of professional actors are rehearsing a play. They are interrupted by six strangers who offer them their life story, help prepare part of a script, and insist on showing them how to act out the roles they help flesh out for the "professional" actors. In the second, a play is being performed before an audience which is also a "player" in the drama, part of the script. The two intermissions carry the stage action into the lobby, where actors continue to perform, the "real" and stage audience mingling, as it were. In the third play, the barrier between the stage and the audience is completely gone; the audience is addressed several times by the Director and actors.

These three plays, *Six Characters* in particular, revolutionized the twentieth-century stage, suggesting prolific possibilities for the future. But in dramatizing the stage *process* and *product* in terms that could be universally applied, in any language, in any theater, Pirandello never lost sight of what he knew best, what had already served him so well in the early plays: the closed society of Sicily, where poverty rules, where there are no outlets for the younger generations, where birth and death, children and property, are the hard realities that define the lives of people trapped in an inhospitable environment, under conditions that suggest the inescapable, harsh restrictions of a caste system.

Critics often shy away from that melodramatic core. Bentley, as we noted earlier, reminds us that Pirandello's ideas might well grow "tiresome." But for the playwright, who was raised in the kind of environment he depicts, among people who elicited his pity and compassion, that life was a dilemma, a paradox deserving attention. He gives that life a literary dimension both in his plays and novels, just as Tennessee Williams, for example, used the South he knew as the background for his plays and F. Scott Fitzgerald used for his fictional settings those places he knew best, including Long Island, New York.

In *Six Characters*, the Sicilian core is the family who suddenly appears out of nowhere, to ask for an author. The group is made up of the Father, the Mother, the Son (oldest of the children and the legitimate offspring of the Father and Mother) the Step-Daughter and two young children — these last three the result of the Mother's union with the man the Father felt was better suited for his wife and forced on her, sending her to live in another town. The Mother, with her new family, returned, destitute, after the other man's death, back where the Father lives with the legitimate son. Somewhere during this period, the Father visits a discreet brothel run by a Madame Pace. He is saved from committing what would have been regarded as incest by the fortuitous revelation that the young woman sent to serve him is the Step-Daughter. The aborted liaison is the crux of the story offered to the professional actors, a story which the Director eventually accepts and which the Father helps to script. The play ends abruptly with the youngest child, a little girl, drowning in a fountain and her young brother shooting himself. This soap-opera scenario is melodramatic indeed but gripping as well. It tells us that what we hold deep inside us is virtually incommunicable: the family members are not satisfied with the "acting" by the professionals and insist they are the only ones who can relay their story on stage, since they have actually lived it. The agony we have witnessed, we must conclude, is an incommunicable "no-exit" situation; the conclusion open-ended, spiraling back to a new beginning, an event destined to be repeated obsessively.

It is also a stunning new vision of a stage

cleared of conventional strategies and turned toward a new horizon. It redefines the relationship between the character and its role, actors and characters, the role of the director, the relationship between actors and audience. All this, as well as the layering of roles, the open-ended conclusion, and the Sicilian "core" story characterize the second theater play, as well. In *Each in His Own Way*, the theater is no longer empty; there is a "scripted" audience watching actors perform a Pirandello play. The two intermissions take place on the stage, following immediately the end of each act, as though they are the actual intermissions one usually enjoys in the back of the theater: an ingenious layered scenario. In the first of the two intermissions, the lovers whose torrid affair and its tragic consequences are the subject of the Pirandello play being performed, run into one another and start quarreling. The "intermission" ends when they run off the stage, and the play resumes. In the second intermission, we witness a confused debate among theater critics commenting on the play they are watching (an exchange that enables Pirandello to criticize in turn the short-sightedness of the would-be theater experts and must have given him great satisfaction to write). When the play resumes, the young woman from the first "intermission" runs on to the stage to protest how she is being depicted. The actors in that stage play, now thoroughly annoyed and frustrated by the interruptions, refuse to continue and walk off: there will be no third act.

In the last of the "theater plays," *Tonight We Improvise*, the audience is once again a "player," addressed on several occasions by the director and actors. (Edward Albee has something very similar to this in *The Man Who Had Three Arms*, where the protagonist is a public speaker addressing an audience in a public hall — which is also the audience in the theater, watching the play.) Pirandello's play has been advertised as an "improvisation" (the playbill, in fact, carries no title) — but we know better, for there has to be a repeatable script if the play is to be performed for more than one night. The play begins with a great deal of shouting and quarreling off stage. The Director comes out several times to apologize for the long delay in getting started. The "improvised" drama finally begins. It centers on a young woman, Mommina, one of three sisters, whose husband is insanely jealous and keeps her a virtual prisoner in her own house. She can't even use a mirror. Just when the young man sees the error of his ways and is ready to free his wife from the unreasonable constraints he has placed on her, the actress playing Mommina suddenly collapses, as though dead. As the audience watches, her fellow-actors come out of their roles to help revive her. The Director, meanwhile, tries to keep the audience calm. (All this, of course, is part of a script.) The play ends with the young woman regaining consciousness, the actors chasing the Director off the stage, explaining to the audience, as they themselves rush off, that they don't need him: they only need . . . a script!

Audiences used to the realistic theater might well ask: Is this a play? Of course: but we must adjust our sights. Theater is now an experience in which we share in an integral way; we can't just sit back and relax. We are watching the shifting kaleidoscopic display of a changing "reality" in which what seems familiar suddenly appears strange, what had been understood becomes uncertain, where paradoxes are the building blocks of the drama. The theater has been turned into the uncertain stage of life, and we are the players. The stage characters, caught in their self-defining moment of awareness, provide us with our cues, how to interpret their doubts. The problem *is* the resolution. The open-ended conclusion of these plays tells us that the experience is a continual one, an experience spiraling toward greater awareness.

In what is considered by many to be his masterpiece, *Enrico IV* (*Henry IV* or *The Emperor Henry IV*, to distinguish him from the English king made famous by Shakespeare), Pirandello gives us what I like to think of as characters who have found their author in the eccentric owner of a villa transformed into an 11th century castle, where servants and anyone coming into his presence must be dressed in the costume of the period — a Hamlet-like protagonist who creates his own drama, rewriting history as well as his own life story. Known only by the identity he has assumed, that of the emperor Enrico IV, the archenemy of Matilda of Tuscany and Pope Gregory VII, the protagonist is visited by a small group, who have come to shock him out of the amnesia he suffered twenty years earlier, as a result of a fall from his horse, while in a costume parade celebrating *mardi gras*. These unexpected visitors are led by the "emperor's" nephew, De Nolli, who has assumed guardianship for the "mad" uncle who has been living in virtual seclusion for twenty years. With him are his uncle's former fiancée, the Marchese Matilda Spina (now middle-aged) and her lover Belcredi; Matilda's daughter Frieda, engaged to De Nolli, a striking younger version of her mother, and a Doctor Genori, a psychiatrist brought along for professional advice. They appear before the "emperor" in the very costumes they wore at the *mardi gras* parade two decades earlier — Frieda in the same gown as her mother, almost a young version of the older woman. De Nolli also appears in costume, a young version of his uncle. The two young people assume statue-like immobility in niches where full-length portraits hang of Matilde and Enrico IV, in the same costumes they wore for the *mardi gras* parade twenty years earlier. This scenario is meant to jolt the amnesiac into the present, mirroring the passage of time; but the plan backfires, for they have no way of knowing that the "emperor" had indeed recovered his memory some years earlier but, not wanting to face a world that had passed him by, did not divulge the fact to anyone. In the chaos that follows their attempt to effect a "cure," the intruders force a *denouement* in which the "emperor" stabs Belcredi, his erstwhile enemy. The fatally wounded man is carried off the stage by the others, in hasty retreat. This turn of events forces the "emperor" to assume his former mask of "madness" as a permanent escape from the unfortunate encounter with his uninvited guests.

In this dizzying pyrotechnic display of roles within roles, of characters assuming and discarding costumes and identities, of a many-layered past; in the protagonist's rewriting of history — a work-in progress, for not only are the historic 11th century events being reinterpreted as he sees fit but also the *mardi gras* parade, when the protagonist, dressed as Enrico IV, fell (or was pushed by his rival) from his horse and suffered the concussion and was diagnosed with permanent amnesia — Pirandello has dramatized for us the dialectical inversions which are the basis of knowledge.

These four plays redefine "reality" by means of a stage drama which is a shifting awareness of the world, clearing us of illusions — the perfect meshing of what Brustein has called the *process* and the *product*. With these plays, Pirandello emerges — in the words of the French critic Georges Neveux — as

> the great prestidigitator of the Twentieth Century, the Houdini of interior life. In his most important play, *Six Characters*, he took the very center of the real world and turned it inside out right in front of us, as the fisherman turns inside out the skin of an octopus to lay bare its viscera.
>
> But what Pirandello laid bare before us is not only the work of the actors, nor that of the author, not only the other side of the scenery, but something much more universal: the other side of ourselves.
>
> It is our inner life which is suddenly found projected on the stage and decomposed there as it by a prism.[9]

What is particularly striking in all this is that Pirandello is able to retain the essentials of a "plot," maintaining the illusion of realism, even as he undermines it.

NOTES

1. Pirandello was keen enough to grasp the potential of the emerging new medium. In May 1930, he wrote: "The future of dramatic art and also of the playwrights is now there — believe me, we must direct ourselves toward a new experience of art: the talking film. I was against it. I changed my mind." He actually wrote a film script called *Shoot! (Si gira!)*

2. Eric Bentley, *The Playwright as Thinker* (World Publishing Co., Cleveland and New York, 1955), p. 148. See also: Paolucci, *Pirandello's Theater: The Recovery of the Modern Stage for Dramatic Art* (Southern Illinois University Press, Carbondale, 1974; rptd Griffon House Publications, Smyrna DE, 2002.. pp. 4, 147.

3. *The Playwright as Thinker*.

4. *Pirandello's Theater:* pp 4-5.

5. *Ibid.*, p. 3.

6. *Ibid.*, p. 5.

7. *On Humor (L'Umorismo)* trans, Antonio Illiano and Daniel P. Testa (University of North Carolina Press, Chapel Hill, 1960) p. 132.

8. *Ibid.*, pp. 136-137.

9. *Pirandello's Theater*, p. 44.

Pirandello and the Waiting Stage of the Absurd (With Some Observations on a New "Critical Language")

In his *Myth of Sisyphus*, Albert Camus defines the feeling that in our time has replaced the security of a "world that can be explained by reasoning, however faulty," as the result of "the divorce between man and his life, the actor and his setting." Lifted from his familiar moorings, "man feels a stranger. His is an irremediable exile. . . ." This existential condition is what "truly constitutes the feeling of Absurdity."[1]

In the more than six decades since those words were written, literature has exploded many myths and has found fertile new ground; and it is hardly surprising that French playwrights should have proved the most consistent in exploring what Camus recognized as the prevailing mood of the post-Second World War age. Theater of the Absurd owes a great deal to Camus; but the man who focused on restructuring the modern stage, bringing to it the sustained energy and innovative talent needed to replace the old Realistic drama, was Luigi Pirandello.

It was Pirandello who first shifted the dramatic sights to the internal fragmented world of the self, forging a new language and a new stage for the purpose. Without him, Theater of the Absurd might not have come into being; it certainly would have taken a different direction. His influence on Sartre, Beckett, Ionesco, Pinter, Albee, Wilder, Gelber, Giraudoux, O'Neill, Camus himself, and so many others, makes him without a doubt "the most seminal dramatist of our time."[2]

A brief version of this essay was read at the Modern Language Association Convention in San Francisco, on December 28, 1979. A fuller version appeared in Modern Drama, *1980. (Slightly revised.)*

Pirandello's existential commitment was not as obvious as Beckett's or as strident as Ionesco's, but it effected major changes in the prevailing realistic theater. He divorced the actor from his traditional posture and prepared him for the dramatic dialectic which was to become the insistent burden of the contemporary theater. He cleared the stage itself of its outworn conventions and restored it to its pristine condition, the *empty potency of the dramatic experience*, to be shaped anew with every new play, like a poem that creates its special language, its unique set of images as it evolves. With this new vision of the stage and its workings, Pirandello restored to theater the old magic of "two boards and a passion." With *Six Characters* in 1921 the full meaning of his changes was made explicit.

In retrospect, we recognize indications of what was to come as early as 1916, with *Liolà*, in which Pirandello sweeps away with a bold reversal of moral polarities a threadbare system of fossilized social and personal responsibilities and unyielding religious habits. The rigorous definitions of his Sicilian society are transformed in that early masterpiece into an implicit question that takes us to the threshold of an existential experience. Against a familiar background, he effects a transvaluation of accepted standards without, paradoxically, demolishing the solid and essential base of the society that is put to a grueling test. The result is not social commentary or a plea for reform but a stripping of the masks we wear to the vulnerable core buried in all of us. Although the protagonists in *Liolà* are realistic, typical even, they already herald the dissolution on stage of the integral character of realistic drama, what will become the signet mark of his art. Within five years of *Liolà*, the conversion of the stage is complete. With his "theater plays," Pirandello dramatizes for us, in a variety of stunning scenarios, shifting relationships, the juxtaposition of masks and roles, the rich dialectic of the unexamined life, facts and illusions, demolishing the external world around us with an incontrovertible and compelling logic. The "theater plays" also move beyond the footlights, oscillating between make-believe and "reality," between the stage and the audience, giving back with each pulse, distorted images as in a crazy mirror, reflections that undermine our assumptions of what we see, who we are, and force us to reexamine the very source of knowledge: the reality of life becomes an illusion and the make-believe of the stage is shown as real, the *process* that enables us to come to terms with ourselves and that can best be described as a spiraling toward the truth. That truth is not always a clear statement. More often than not, it eludes us, coming to light as an unanswered question — an awareness that is a truth in itself, a factor in the final equation.

Pirandello recognized in the spiraling toward definition the energizing content for his restructured stage. It is a stage in constant flux, on which we watch the traumatic dissolution of character into attitudes, states of being, moments of awareness.

In *Six Characters*, Pirandello give us the first explicit clue as to the function of the "mask" in his new theater and the kinds of adjustments we, as audience, as potential "masks," must make to engage actively in the dramatic exchange. "Engagement" in this context is neither optional nor arbitrary; it is part of the organic experience and cannot be avoided. From this time on, the audience will never again be excused from contributing to the process of the stage experience. It will do so imperceptibly, almost without realizing what has happened.

The point of all this is to get rid of everything that is holding us down, keeping us from realizing the true self. The facts, assumptions, and prejudices we accept without question must be abandoned for an organic whole to emerge, one that corresponds to our inner being. The Pirandellian dialectic is not a simple opposition leading to statement and conversion but a kaleidoscopic mosaic of purpose and consistency. The protagonist in this kind of setting is a stratification of moments, a voice for contradictory emotions and intentions.

In this kind of fragmented, constantly evolving stage, endings are abrupt: action comes to a standstill, the stage business interrupted or cut short, and (especially in the "theater plays" and *Enrico IV*) the actors abandon their roles to rush off into the darkness of an abortive ending.

In its potential as an active participant in this dramatic process, the audience provides a bridge between the compelling "illusion" of the stage and the unsubstantial "reality" waiting to be reshaped. *Six Characters* gives us the outer layer of awareness, following the cues of the stage actors, whose responses anticipate and correspond to those of the audience. *Each in His Own Way* shows the audience on two levels of awareness: it is a "player," watching the stage play, as well as the audience in the theater. The audience in *Tonight We Improvise* is the same audience, on two levels at once, addressed by the actors and the Director on several occasions and echoing in their reactions the responses on stage.

These three "theater plays" are a progressive sequence which contains most of the characteristics that have come to be associated with "Theater of the Absurd": the telescoping of time that superimposes disparate psychological moments on to a "realistic" chronological base; an inexorable dialectic that shatters assumptions and erodes the external world that remains outside us; a structure built on paradoxes that jolt us out of complacency and force us into questioning and doubt. In later plays, Pirandello will continue this journey into the interior, showing us that it is more than a stage play. We are led into the realization that the stage is no longer *imitation* of life but the *creation of a reconstituted reality*, based on the certainty inside us, which defines our place and purpose in that reality. In this new setting, the stage is also the moment of conversion that enables us to free ourselves from the formal postures and masks that hide us from our true selves.

Such changes mandate a new critical language; old guidelines no longer work. Objective correlatives and critical evaluations based on the familiar Aristotelian categories will simply lead us astray if applied here. Those categories should never be forgotten; but Aristotle himself would have been the first to recognize their limitations in our age, as Hegel, the modern Aristotle, did in fact, when he put forward the genial notion that in our age, when "spirit" has come to know itself in the full freedom of knowledge of self, "art transcends itself."[3]

How does one discuss action, character, theme, and language — the critical catagories that have served so well for two millenia — in dealing with plays that circle around a core, that do not move to a resolution but end arbitrarily, often abruptly; where characters are not integral idiosyncratic personalities but "voices" that express obsessive concerns, attitudes, moments of recognition and awareness; where theme, if considered at all, is far removed from the "message" plays of Chekhov or Arthur Miller; where language is made up of paradoxes, repetitions, refrains and echoes, expressions of a splintered consciousness trying to piece together the shards of experience?

Theater critics on the whole have skirted the challenge but some recent criticism has in fact gravitated toward an Hegelian interpretation of dramatic realities that take us to the edge of non-theater and exceed existing definitions or — in Hegel's words — take us to a new level of critical awareness, where, as we already had occasion to mention, "art transcends itself." One scholar who has insisted on the need for a new language to deal with the Absurd is Vivian Mercier. The very title of his excellent study, *Beckett/Beckett* — suggests a dialectical approach, a language of inversions and paradoxes. In his preface to the book, Mercier recalls the response of the audience at a symposium which followed a performance of

Waiting for Godot. Someone asked: Isn't *Waiting for Godot* a sort of Rorschach test?" The speaker, we are told, was clapped and cheered by most of those present, who clearly felt that most interpretations of that play — indeed of Samuel Beckett's work as a whole — reveal more about the psyche of the people who offer them than about the work itself or the psyche of its author."[4] Well, yes: every response to a true work of art expands as the reader's interests expand. More to the point: Pirandello expects his audience to respond in a profound and personal way, but not as an arbitrary reaction, different for each individual. The Rorschach test is the moment of abstract atomistic response, the casual mirror image thrown back to us. How do we turn that first awareness of a new consciousness into the infinite reflection of self-consciousness mirroring back "one, no one, a hundred thousand"? How does one reach for definition, when the very language used has to be created from scratch? How does one find the proper terms to explain the shaping of art out of chaos?

Mercier sees the answer in the *dialectic* (using the term in a generic sense and never referring to Hegel). The very structure of the new theater calls for a language that will reflect adequately the new language of the Absurd. David H. Hesla reminds us that "the shape of Beckett's art is the shape of the dialectic" — a synthesis of positive and negative, comedy and pathos, the yes and the no, optimism and pessimism, hope and despair. Mercier sets up his chapter heads as paradoxes: "Ireland / The World," "Ear / Eye," "Gentleman / Tramp," "Classicism / Absurdism," etc. Beckett criticism, he observes, is "somewhat aware of each dialectic," but it tends to "emphasize one of the poles to the almost total negation of the other."[5]

What Mercier succeeds in doing is revitalize the Hegelian notion of the transcendence of art and the fully sensitized "beautiful soul" (*schöne Seele*) as the most effective critical elements for an understanding of the Absurd, a theater which verges, as we already said, on non-theater. Of course, Mercier reminds us, so long as the playwright continues to write, he will not, "in this life at least . . . reach either silence or nothingness." What we have (and Beckett is an excellent example) is "a dialectic . . . between silence and garrulity."[6] And, like all dialectical inversions, the two elements are intimately related: in their relationship they emerge as both distinct and identical. The "garrulity" of Beckett's "anti-heroes," like that of Hamlet and so many of the Pirandellian protagonists, is the other side of silence. One of the best examples is Edward Albee's *Quotations from Chairman Mao and Box*, where the people on stage indulge in private monologues, addressing not so much the audience as their own consciousness. Pirandello's open-ended arguments offer a similar dialectic.

Martin Esslin was among the first to recognize in the Absurd "a gradual devaluation of language . . . a poetry that is to emerge from the concrete and objectified images of the stage itself." Language "still plays an important part . . . but what *happens* on the stage transcends, and often contradicts, the *words* spoken by the characters."[7]

Mercier's study of Beckett's dramatic art is the first consistent effort to probe the dialectic of the Absurd in critical terms. It reminds us, among other things, that to look for "objective correlatives" in a writer whose work is not so much themes as "fundamental sounds" (Beckett's own phrase)[8] is to miss what is characteristically Absurd. And what has been said of Beckett applies, of course, to other playwrights who work in a medium where irony is the familiar score, definition is by exclusion, explicit statement is avoided. The following description of Beckett's dramatic language could just as well be applied to Pirandello, for example. It is the language

> . . . of man talking to himself, in the first place the author, and in the second place each individual member of the audience: and this "outer" language between the stage and the audience extends also to the

"inner" language of the stage itself, where the characters too are men and women talking to themselves. Beckett tells himself a story in the form of a play, each member of the audience tells himself the story in the form of Beckett's play, and within the play the characters tell themselves stories. What is on the stage is not only the occasion for the content of the dialogue with the audience, it is also a metaphor, an image of the dialogue between the author and himself as audience, between the member of the audience and himself as author.[9]

The Pirandellian world is an expanding experience of the same kind. The concentric, ever-widening areas of correspondences Mercier defines for Beckett are found also and first in Pirandello, especially in the "theater plays" and *Enrico IV*, where for the first time the stage becomes our own consciousness of the latent drama in us all.

NOTES

1. Albert Camus, *Le Mythe de Sisyphe* (Paris, 1942. Cited by Martin Esslin, *The Theater of the Absurd* (New York, 1961), p. xix.

2. Robert Brustein, *The Theater of Revolt* (Boston, 1964), pp. 316-317. See also, Anne Paolucci, *Pirandello's Theater: The Recovery of the Modern Stage for Dramatic Art* (Southern Illinois University Press, Carbonville, Ill., 1974), pp. 4-5.

3. Anne and Henry Paolucci, *Hegel on Tragegy* (Doubleday Co., New York, 1962), p. xxi. Rptd Harper and Row (1974), Greenwood Press (hbd 1978), Griffon House Publications (2001).

4. Vivian Mercier, *Beckett/Beckett* (New York, 1977), p. vii.

5. *Ibid.*, p. 11.

6. *Ibid.*, p. 18.

7. Esslin, p. xxi.

8. Mercier, p. 18.

9. John Fletcher and John Sparling, *Beckett: A Study of His Plays* (London, 1972), pp. 37-38.

BENTLEY ON PIRANDELLO:
FORTY YEARS LATER

Before the appearance of *The Playwright as Thinker*,[1] there was little in the literature on Pirandello to make one pause and take notice. It seemed ironic that the truly new exciting assessment in English about the 1934 Italian Nobel Prize Laureate in Literature should come from a critic who was neither Italian nor an academic. Those who followed in his tracks, like Francis Fergusson and Robert Brustein, were also non-Italian. Critics writing in Italian had dealt with Pirandello's work all along, of course, but using the traditional categories, trying to fit into them action that often circled in a loop and seemed to go nowhere, characters who eluded definition, themes that were anything but clear, and a language that was often built on paradoxes.

In other words: until Bentley, critics for the most part had missed the point; Pirandello's novelties eluded standard interpretation; the very things that made him strikingly new were often seen as excesses (*e.g.* too "cerebral," etc.). Bentley was the first to give Pirandello immediate standing as a playwright who was innovative and creative in a way that defied familiar critical molds. He placed him within the spectrum of European drama, which was already far ahead of us. By focusing on Pirandello's revolutionary handling of the stage, Bentley provided the best possible introduction to the Sicilian playwright.

For the first time Pirandello, who had changed forever European drama more than a generation earlier with the production of *Six Characters in Search of an Author*, staged in Paris by Georges and Ludmilla

---

Written for a collection of essays, The Play and its Critics, *in honor of Eric Bentley, edited by Michael Bertin (University Press of America, 1986), pp. 113-121. (Slightly revised.)*

Pitoëff in 1923, was brought to the attention of the American public. It was an important development but with limited impact, since most American critics and scholars — still burdened with a Realistic theater — were not sure how to deal with it. Pirandello himself had visited the United States a few years before his death, to promote his plays, but that effort too had no lasting effect.

In spite of a limited audience, Bentley's assessment provided the foundations on which future critics were to build. He examined Pirandello's work in unassailable terms, comparing it often with other modern playwrights — comments that are still fresh and intriguing, even at a distance of forty years.

In the few paragraphs devoted to Pirandello, Bentley isolates the playwright's single most important feature, "the quintessence of Pirandellism," as the "peculiar relation of intellect to feeling." He knocks down the charge of "cerebral," explaining how the Pirandello translates argument into immediate human responses. He dismisses the constantly repeated critical notion of "relativity," insisting that it "be set on one side," that "it is not [the playwright's] business to uncover the problem and solve it for us."[2]

How different from the metaphysical and other esoteric arguments used for and against Pirandello by so many critics and scholars! Bentley tears away the heavy critical scaffolding favored by academics and has shown us how to *feel* the novelty of Pirandello's plays. He is not afraid of unconventional strategies and ignores a critical language that no longer works. He levels the familiar charge of *pessimism,* so often raised against the playwright, in words that force the reader's attention into a new direction, creating a new kind of critical metaphor that will jolt us out of any conventional assessment:

> What a pessimist Pirandello is! says someone. Certainly. But again the point of Pirandello is not his philosophy — of relativity, personality, or pessimism — it is his power to conceal behind the intellectual artillery

barrage the great armies of fighters and the yet greater hordes of noncombatants and refugees. Pirandello is a pessimist. So also must many of the people of Europe be, people who have lived through the extraordinary vicissitudes of the twentieth century, uncomprehending, passively suffering. . . . Pirandello, like Kafka, like Chaplin, speaks not for the aware and class-conscious proletarian but for the unaware, in-between, black-white-cotton-coated scapegoat.[3]

In the last two and a half pages of the eight pages devoted to Pirandello, Bentley departs even more radically from conventional criticism and provides us with a "note to the director [of *Right You Are! [If You Think So]*]," which is more enlightening that anything that could be offered in a straightforward critical appraisal:

> Make a marked distinction between the enquirers into the story, who are a sort of chorus representing what Pirandello regards as the Mask and the three "real People" involved in the domestic tragedy. The Three are typical people of a middle-class tragedy in that they express grief and arouse pity without terror. Note how Pirandello's initial description of the characters and his subsequent stage directions stress alike the genuineness and acuteness of their sufferings.[4]

He underscores — still as improvised stage directions — the need to bring out laughter "when perhaps weeping would seem more in order." The old theatrical business of "mingling laughter and tears was never more calculated, more intricate, more meaningful, or more depressing than here" — a description in keeping with Pirandello's definition of humor as *il sentimento del contrario*.[5] The director must focus, finally, on the dialectical form of the play.

> Accentuate then — do not soften — the clashes of sound and color of which the play is composed. If you let it work, you will find the whole thing ultratheatrical."[6]

By not submitting to the programmed analyses which served so well the Realistic theater introduced by Ibsen, Chekhov, Strindberg, perfected in the United States by Eugene O'Neill, continued by many of our playwrights, right down to Arthur Miller and beyond; by recognizing the crucial need for a critical language that would do justice to plays like Pirandello's; by forcing us to view the Pirandellian stage as virgin territory, waiting to be discovered; Bentley gave Pirandellian studies a totally new direction.

I followed that direction in my book on Pirandello,[7] where I examined the plays from a number of angles, comparing *Enrico IV* to Shakespeare's *Hamlet* and looking at the "theater plays" from the perspective of the Absurd. I noted affinities with Beckett and Ionesco, recognized allegorical resonances similar to those found in the plays of Edward Albee (*viz.*, *The Zoo Story*, *Who's Afraid of Virginia Woolf?*, *Tiny Alice*, etc.), struggled with concepts which at the time were essentially gut reactions, and came to realize that Pirandello was at the very center of the contemporary theater, its prime instigator, in fact.

The concept of "non-theater" continued to intrigue me, especially after reading Vivian Mercier's compelling argument in *Beckett/Beckett*, where he makes clear the need for a new "dialectical" critical language for the Absurd. I also came to understand how this new theater, verging on non-theater, answered the provocative and still little-understood Hegelian notion of "art transcending itself" in the modern world, where the spirit has come into its own in the fullness of individual freedom.[8] I also realized that although my book had merely scratched the surface, Bentley had given me the assurance I needed to continue my studies on Pirandello, a playwright who many critics still regard as a figure of the past, without contemporary relevance and, by some misguided souls, as an "ethnic" author!

I had learned to value Bentley's judgment, having worked with him over the years. He had asked me in the sixties to translate as the introduction to *The Genius of the Italian Theater*,[9] Pirandello's brilliant essay on the history of the Italian theater — a gem that Bentley understood should be made available in English and which I undertook only at his insistence. Our earliest communication was in connection with a translation my husband and I were preparing of Machiavelli's dramatic masterpiece, *Mandragola*, the first new translation since Stark Young's, twenty-five years earlier. He wanted it for an anthology he was preparing, but we had already agreed to publish our translation with The Liberal Arts Press.

Since *The Playwright as Thinker*, Bentley has written much else on theater and Pirandello. His collection of essays, published in 1985 under the title *Pirandellian Studies I*, brings together samplings that cover four decades of critical writings (1946-1985), including an original Bentley version of *Enrico IV* set on Long Island with the title *H for Hamlet*.[10] He obviously has survived the fads and special interests that plague so much critical writing — Freudian, Marxist, etc. Like T. S. Eliot and A. C. Bradley (two of the most provocative and readable critics in English), Bentley gives the reader the impression of travelling the distance with him, of discovering in the best Socratic tradition what is true — not by statement but by paradoxical analysis and query. It is the kind of criticism that lives and communicates beyond its time.

Enough has been said to convince the reader that from the very beginning Bentley hit on the essentials of Pirandello's theater and was able to get the message across. He went further, as we know, taking on the important (if often thankless) task of making available translations of Pirandello's major plays for his volume, *Naked Masks*.[11] The picture that emerges is of a truly dedicated critic, one whose vision and language has brought us much closer to Pirandello's world.

Pirandello admired innovation. He respected leaps of genius, what others might have construed as aberrations. In his essay on the history of the Italian theater,[12] he describes his lucid vision of the central role played by the Italian theater as it moved from religious forms to the living (if still somewhat crude) forms of a natural environment. He cites Boccaccio and reviews the spirit of "romance" that found its way into the Italian theater at that time, giving it, among other things, "a sense of movement." But it is Goldoni, he tells us in no uncertain terms, who was the first to build entire plays around secondary characters like Mirandolina in *La locanderia* (*Mistress of the Inn*), thus preparing the European theater for Molière and others. Like Pirandello focusing on the important changes brought about by Goldoni, Bentley has given us a memorable critique of Pirandello's new theater.

NOTES

1. Eric Bentley, *The Playwright as Thinker* (World Publishing Co., Meridian Books, New York, 1946).

2. *Ibid.*, pp. 148-149.

3. *Ibid.*, p. 151.

4. *Ibid.*, pp. 151-152.

5. See, *L'Umorismo, On Humor*, trans. Antonio Illiano and Daniel P. Testa (University of North Carolina Press, Chapel Hill, **1965**).

6. Bentley, *op. cit.*, p. 153.

7. Anne Paolucci, *Pirandello's Theater: The Recovery of the Modern Stage for Dramatic Art* (Southern Illinois University Press, Carbondale, 1974); rptd Griffon House Publications. Smytna, DE, 2002).

8. See, Anne and Henry Paolucci, *Hegel on Tragedy* (Doubleday & Co, New York, 1962; rptd Harper and Row [1974], Greenwood Press [1978], Griffon House Publications [2001]).

9. "Pirandello's Introduction to the Italian Theater," tran. Anne Paolucci, *The Genius of the Italian Theater*, ed Eric Bentley (Mentor Books, The New American Library, New York, 1964), pp. 11-29.

10. Walter J. Centuori, ed., *Pirandellian Studies I* (University of Nebraska Press, Lincoln, 1985).

11. Eric Bentley, ed. *Naked Masks* (E. P. Dutton & Co., Inc., New York, 1952.

12. "Pirandello's Introduction to the Italian Theater."

PART TWO
CRITICAL ANALYSES

RESEARCH NOTES

- Computer scientists make robot perform checker-playing tasks
- Molecular analysis links coelacanth to first terrestrial vertebrate
- Themes of Pirandello's plays are seen in earlier works of fiction
- Effects of divorce on children said to occur before parents split

Notes on Research: Plays of Pirandello

Themes explored in the plays of Luigi Pirandello were introduced by the author in earlier works of fiction, says a literature scholar at St. John's University in New York.

Pirandello, the Italian playwright and novelist who died in 1936, is best known for his 1921 experimental drama, *Six Characters in Search of an Author.* The play takes place on a stage on which actors are gathering for rehearsal. Six people arrive at the theater, claiming that they are unfinished creations of the author's imagination and demanding to be allowed to play out their personal dramas on the stage. Their stories then unfold, as the lines between actors and "real" characters become increasingly blurred.

In the current (March) issue of *Modern Drama,* Anne Paolucci, head of the English department at St. John's, notes that, until he wrote *Six Characters,* Pirandello's reputation had rested largely on a body of fiction that depicted in realistic terms the harshness of Sicilian life. But with the play, and others that followed, he began to explore a new kind of theme—the interior search for identity and how that search can liberate a person from the constraints of the environment.

Ms. Paolucci argues that the themes of Pirandello's plays, written later in his career, were actually announced in some of the earlier fiction. His 1904 novel, *The Late Mattia Pascal,* for example, is the story of a man who, returning from a solitary holiday, reads a mistaken announcement of his own suicide. He takes the error as an opportunity to escape his old life and begin a new existence. He finds his new life even more constraining, however, and fakes a second suicide in order to return to his earlier existence, albeit on different terms.

The novel, Ms. Paolucci argues, was Pirandello's first direct expression of a pessimistic view of humans trapped by hostile forces but overcoming that condition through their gradually evolving sense of identity and consciousness of freedom.

—ELLEN K. COUGHLIN

SICILIAN THEMES AND THE RESTRUCTURED STAGE: THE DIALECTIC OF FICTION AND DRAMA IN THE WORK OF LUIGI PIRANDELLO

When, in 1923, at the age of 56, Pirandello won European acclaim with the Pitoëff production *of Six Characters in Search of an Author* (the same play that had been booed off the stage and had caused a riot at its premiere in Rome two years earlier), he had already published six of his seven novels, several volumes of short stories, and four volumes of poetry. His reputation as a writer of fiction was firmly established when he turned to drama; and although he never gave up writing fiction — and was to convert many of his short stories into plays in the years that followed — by 1923 he had clearly shifted his sights. For the rest of his life, his artistic priorities were to be focused on drama.

It was in 1916 that Pirandello realized his potential as a dramatist, with the recognition received for two plays written in the dialect of his native Agrigento, in Sicily: *Pensaci, Giacomino! (Think it over, Jamie!)* and the genial *Liolà* — both written for the renowned Sicilian actor Angelo Musco. These early plays reflect the *verismo* of his already mature fiction; later works will continue to depict in a variety of ways the realism made popular in Italy at the time by other Sicilian writers like Giovanni Verga and Antonio Fogazzaro: a deep-rooted interest in the closed society of southern Italy, where rigorous self-protective conventions, shaped by dire poverty and isolation, cannot be subverted without risking one's life and loved ones; where "real" values prevail — property, land, the things that count, so hard to come by in such a land.

Women suffer the most. They can't break away from such a prescribed existence, without bringing dis-

---

First appeared in Modern Drama, *Vol. XXXIV, No. 1, March 1991, pp. 138-147. (Slightly revised.)*

astrous results on both themselves and those close to them. And where marriages are rooted in economic necessity, women serve as pawns to insure security, financial stability, or simple survival.

The silent suffering of women in this closed society, the ostracized rebels who cannot escape their fate even away from the source of their troubles, the inescapable destinies of the poor, the bonds that trap the rich, the entire spectrum of Sicilian attitudes and values to which all must subscribe— all these are a compelling reality not only in Pirandello's fiction but also in his plays.

The sorry condition of women in this barren land is a constant theme. Some, trapped by their passions are driven to destruction by their unfulfilled ambitions (Tuzza in *Liolà*). Others become victims of their own ambitions when they try to find place and success in a cosmopolitan environment (*Lumie di Sicilia*). Still others are driven to desperate measures in the face of irreversible, inescapable events dictated by conditions beyond their control (The Mother, the Step-Daughter, in *Six Characters*; Mita in *Liolà*). Even in the "theater plays" that made him an international avant-garde sensation as a playwright, Pirandello insists on a Sicilian "core" narrative, in which women are shown undergoing severe emotional ordeals.

In depicting the erosion of the soul within the Sicilian setting which he loved, criticized, and rejected with difficulty, Pirandello displayed, both in his fiction and his drama, the kind of genial combination of "strong local colour" and "unconscious universality" which — according to T. S. Eliot — is the sure sign of greatness in a new, "untried" author.[1] Pirandello's fiction and much of his drama are rooted in this paradox. As a playwright, however, he soon hit on a new and powerful subject, perhaps the inevitable result of focusing on the lives of people living in a barren place, where nature herself is hostile and the individual a victim without reprieve. His earliest plays as well as his novels and short stories examine the effects of such an existence in the most detailed way; but by 1921, with *Six Characters*, he turned with even greater fascination to exploring *personality* in its conscious and deliberate effort to come to terms with the outside world. We watch, in *Six Characters*, as this new obsession is translated powerfully into a stage language itself new and overwhelming. The Sicilian story is there, still, but only as a motive for examining the experience outside itself, outside its local habitation, against the conventions and prejudices of another kind of life and commitment.

The stage itself becomes a living character in this extraordinary confrontation, and the actors move in and of "real" and "stage" roles in a telescopic oscillation that forever destroyed the notion of stage and audience as distinct and mutually exclusive realities. With the "theater plays," Pirandello found the medium and language of redemption for the damned souls of his closed society. By exploring the maze of its own consciousness, personality could free itself from the bonds of external necessity — a liberating process, regardless of the result: for in defining one's limits, the struggle toward identity also points to forces within us, waiting to be tapped.

The "theater plays" announce this new and exciting direction in the most vivid terms; and they make clear at the same time that the search for identity is a most promising subject for the new drama of existential emotions and avant-garde techniques. Robert Brustein rightly insists that Pirandello hit on something truly extraordinary: his new vision of the stage intrigued and inspired just about every major playwright of our time.[2]

In a rush of inspiration, Pirandello wrote, in a short span of three years, the four plays that would revolutionize the European and world theater and set it on a new, totally unexpected course for decades to come. In *Six Characters, Each in His Own Way, Tonight We Improvise* and *Enrico IV*, Pirandello discovered not only his own potential as a playwright but in the process also rediscovered the true potential of the stage. Drama, he made stunningly clear, was a *continuum*, a constant *becoming*. He used telescopic techniques to destroy the passive notion of static "illusion" on stage, superimposing levels of action, moving actors in and out of their "formal" roles, juxtaposing "real" events with stage plots, creating a dialectic spiraling of masks within masks, settings within settings, realities within realities. In the fragmentation that resulted, a new force was unleashed that was to revitalize both drama and fiction in the years to come.

The first indication of Pirandello's growing interest in exploring the inner world of personality as it seeks organic identity is to be found in the early novel, *Il fù Mattia Pascal (The Late Mattia Pascal)*, written in 1904. The work has puzzled some critics who would like to see a straight-line development from early but fully articulated examples of a major theme to later writings, especially the "theater plays." Critics like Renato Barilli, for example, see this novel as out of sequence, for Pirandello's second novel, the much longer *I Vecchi e i giovani (The Old and the Young)* reverts to the heavy Sicilian inspiration of his very early works, like *L'Esclusa (The Outcast)*, and the rich and traditional inspiration of the realistic regional novels of Verga, Fogazzaro, and — in the case of *L'Esclusa* — of Luigi Capuana.[3] Barilli in fact deals with *I Vecchi e i giovani* out of sequence in his critical analysis of Pirandello's fiction. Yet, even in this large clearly historical panorama of the dire effects of Italian unification on Southern Italy — a rich and complex canvas not unlike that of Lampedusa's *Il Gattopardo (The Leopard)* — Pirandello has occasion to trace the complicated and often contradictory motives and intentions that have already taken root in his plays. The Sicily that is forgotten in the wake of Italian "unity," that is betrayed, abandoned, left to its grim future by the politicians in Rome, intoxicated with their new power as leaders of the late-comer into the family of European nations, is itself a character waiting to be redefined, rediscovered, restructured, redeemed. In drawing this rich and complex canvas, he shows us the poor people of Sicily caught in political realities not much different from the Camus-type trap in which Mattia Pascal or the mad "emperor" Enrico IV find themselves. Even "out of sequence," *I Vecchi e i giovani* is surprisingly consistent with Pirandello's later works in depicting the struggle between oppression and freedom, the existential frustrations and despair people suffer in the face of unrelenting hostile forces. The realities of history honed both his narrative and his dramatic art.

It is also true, however, that in the strange story of *Il fù Mattia Pascal* stages of consciousness and the search for identity are given a surprisingly mature form at a very early date. The spiraling dialectic of escape and return, rejection and acceptance, the end circling back to the beginning in a paradoxical tragic-ironic-humorous conclusion, is as dizzying as the layering of roles in *Six Characters*, seventeen years later. The same forces that were to shape his theater had already found fertile ground in Pirandello's early fiction.

The protagonist of this early novel has been called "a fugitive from life,"[4] but he is more properly a magician creating his own illusions and, as always in Pirandello, rejecting them in the end. The story contains elements of gross improbability, but Pirandello somehow makes them believable. Mattia Pascal, seeking an opportunity to vacation alone and escape his wife's nagging, visits Monte Carlo, where he wins a great deal of money. On his way home, he reads an account of his "death" — ruled by the authorities a suicide by drowning. The body has been identified by his wife and others who knew him.

Pascal views this as a sign, an intervention from the powers that be, and accepts the bizarre turn of events as an opportunity to start his life anew. Under the assumed name of Adriano Meis, he proceeds to travel throughout northern Italy, but in time he is once again caught in the familiar tendrils of personal relationships and social commitments and realizes he has not escaped very far, after all. The new life he has forged for himself is not only similar to the one he fled but adds to his difficulties, since his new identity cannot be legally recognized. With the realization that he has in fact created a new trap for himself, he stages a second "suicide," leaving behind his hat, cane, and a signed note on the parapet of a bridge along the Tiber, before returning to Sicily. There he finds that his "widow" has remarried and has a new family. Not fazed by the problems created by his return (not the least of which is the illegitimate status of his wife's child by the man she thought she had been free to marry after her husband "drowned"), Pascal returns to his job as town librarian and dedicates himself to writing about his experience.

Almost two decades later, the novel still seemed far-fetched to many readers. For the 1921 Mondadori edition, Pirandello included an appendix, in which he explained the contradictions "between reality and imagination" and cited a notice which had appeared in one of the leading Italian papers some months earlier about a man "who had visited his own grave."[5] This is the very year that *Six Characters* was booed off stage, no doubt because of its implausible core story of what was regarded as incest but also, very likely, because of its unfamiliar and (for most) unsatisfying, structure. In spite of its unconventional "redemption" of values, however, the novel won wide recognition when it was published by the firm of Treves. This was indeed an achievement, at a time when Verga was still unappreciated and D'Annunzio was the great literary light of Italy. According to Douglas Radcliff-Umstead, the success of *Il fù Mattia Pascal* was due in large part to Pirandello's "effort to move beyond the Veristic preoccupation with the problems of life in a closed provincial town." The novel "represented precisely the desire to escape enslavement within a society through the construction of a wholly original personality,"[6] Gaspare Giudice goes even further:

> It was probably in the very writing of *Il fù Mattia Pascal* that Pirandellian fiction, until then searching for objective correlatives, works its way with greater assurance into the conscience, becomes introspective, making careful distinctions within the context of a special kind of subjective humor. . . . One finds in it what amounts to an enjoyment of misery, a flash of intuition that takes sour delight in feeling out a newfound wound that has not yet begun to fester.[7]

Il fù Mattia Pascal is the first clear statement of a theme rooted in a pessimistic view of man trapped by hostile forces but rising out of that condition by a slowly evolving consciousness of freedom — a theme richly suggesting a cyclical return to a basically unchanged beginning, which is to say, the dialectic of escape and return with all its ironic suggestivity, roles within roles, ironic parallels often superimposed (the first accidental "suicide" and the deliberately staged "suicide"), a special brand of humor (the perverse decision at the end not to cancel the "death certificate"), paradoxes (committing "suicide" in order to be restored to life), multilayered self-evaluations and self-analyses, restructuring past events according to one's ideal vision of the experience, after settling back in, etc. etc.

With *Six Characters*, the paradoxical core story, full of unexpected twists, is now part of a larger setting. It has been forced to retreat somewhat, to allow for a more immediate dramatic concern: the bringing together of both the illusion of life and the reality of the stage. In this new format, escape is also freedom from stage conventions, from traditional forms, from a formal language to a language of intense natural emotion, and so on. There is nothing uncertain about this first "theater play," nothing "experimental" about it. In its fragmented, kaleidoscopic structure, it mirrors back our own contradictory attitudes and emotions, sets into motion our doubts and uncertainties, reduces everything that is usually taken for granted to doubt and provocative questions.

But even before *Six Characters*, Pirandello had found a way of bringing the novelties of *Il fù Mattia Pascal* into the theater. As early as 1917, with *Così è (Se Vi pare) (Right You Are! [If You Think So])*, only a year after *Liolà*, Pirandello had succeeded in translating for the stage the illusion of "facts," the uncertainties of the objective world around us, the need to redefine "reality" in our own terms in order to accept it. He himself acknowledged the stunning discovery, the new stage he had created. Writing to his son about it, he cannot conceal his excitement:

> It's a great piece of devilish mischief . . . bursting with originality.[8] (My translation)

The play was adapted from one of his own short stories, but echoes of *Il fù Mattia Pascal* are also discernible. The plot relies heavily on familiar elements: implausible situations, a grotesque convergence of far-fetched and yet fully admissible events, the demolition of facts, etc.

The plot is ingenious. Signora Ponza's identity is in question because of contradictory assertions made by her husband and Signora Frola, who identifies herself as the young woman's mother. Ponza is called in by his new employer, Councilman Agazzi, a prominent small town politician, to explain things, ostensibly to curb rumors but really to satisfy the morbid curiosity being fueled by the strange living arrangement of the three newcomers in town: why Ponza has set up his mother-in-law just down the hall from the Agazzis, in an expensive apartment, while he and his wife live on the top floor of an old walk-up on the outskirts of town.

But before Ponza arrives, Signora Frola hurries in from down the hall, ostensibly to pay the usual visit protocol calls for. When pressed, she tells Agazzi and his friends that her poor son-in-law believes that his wife (Signora Frola's daugher) died and that he has since remarried, a second wife. Signora Frola has gone along with the fiction, to spare the poor man unnecessary grief. They even had to go through a mock ceremony, so he would take back his wife, now fully recovered. He is obsessively protective of her, which explains the living arrangements and why Signora Frola is not allowed to get too close to her.

Her audience is stunned, commiserates with her. After she leaves, Ponza arrives with a completely different account, which contradicts Signora Frola's version. He keeps the two women apart — he tells his listeners — because Signora Frola believes her daughter to be still alive, to have recovered after an illness which, in fact, claimed her life. Ponza's new wife is a completely different woman; but Signora Frola, after a breakdown that forced Ponza to put her in a nursing home, suddenly regains her health one day, when she spots Ponza with his new wife and jumps to the conclusion that her daughter, now fully restored to health, is now back with her husband. For his mother-in-law's sake, Ponza has allowed her to harbor the delusion; it's the only way she can be spared the grief and depression that the girl's death had brought on. For Signora Frola is still mad with grief, Ponza tells them, and his obligation is to protect her. Of course, he has had to make sure that the two women never meet face to face.

Almost on cue, Signora Fronza turns up again, right after Ponza leaves, to disclaim her son-in-law's account of things, a story with which she seems to be thoroughly familiar. To convince her audience, she repeats in detail what Ponza has just told them. By the time she leaves again, the others are convinced that it's Ponza who's crazy.

All along, Laudisi, Agazzi's brother-in-law, has been warning the assembled friends and neighbors that their search for "facts" will lead them no where. The "facts," actually, have been wiped out by a massive earthquake that leveled the town of Marsica, where the three newcomers came from. They were the only survivors; no one is left to tell the world who the woman married to Ponza really is, except, of course, the woman herself. But when she is finally brought in, she is heavily veiled, and all she can tell them is that she is Signora Frola's daughter and Ponza's second wife. In herself, she is no one. For others, she is what they make her out to be.

Così è (se vi pare) is the brilliant prelude to the "theater plays." The transformations described in Pirandello's first novel, *Il fù Mattia Pascal*, are seen as shifting identities in this early transitional play. Laudisi, the probing skeptic who turns everything upside down, is the catalyst who dismantles what is commonly accepted as "reality," reducing what appears obvious to an illusion. He destroys the dichotomy between the inner and outer world, but he himself remains a double image, a mirrored reflection, not to be confounded — as so many critics have — with Pirandello's view of things. The dichotomy we see dramatized here is not the answer but the terms of the equation. The answer lies within us. Laudisi's suggestion of "relativity" is the aborted truth. To arrive at "truth," the outer world must be translated into an interior experience, subjective correlatives. "Facts" are not self-evident. So long as they remain outside us as unexamined "givens," automatically accepted, we are in the limbo of uncertainty and chaos.

The "theater plays" are proof of the symbiosis achieved by Pirandello between the illusion of life and the reality of the stage. *Six Characters* is a kaleidoscope of shifting images: masks and characters who profess to be "real" people; actors who are trying to assume those roles; actors creating a script dictated by the "real" people; the stage itself in flux as the life drama is measured against a tentative script, the illusion of improvisation interrupted by the "professionals" who need that script; dramatic action pushed into the background and finally truncated. In this play, the stage is turned into a multi-layered experience, the boundaries of "real life" and dramatic illusion strained to the edge of "non-theater" — or, to use a different image, the stage becomes a series of expanding concentric circles, reaching out into the audience and beyond.

NOTES

1. T. S. Eliot, "American Literature and the American Language," *To Criticize the Critic* (New York, 1965), p. 54.

2. Robert Brustein, "Pirandello's Drama of Revolt," in *Pirandello: A Collection of Critical Essays*, ed. Glauco Cambon (Englewood Cliffs, N.J., 1967), p. 133. See also: Anne Paolucci, *Pirandello's Theater: The Recovery of the Modern Stage for Dramatic Art* (Southern Illinois University Press, Carbondale, 1974), pp. 4-5.

3. Renato Barilli, *La Linea Svevo-Pirandello* (Milano, 1977), pp. 153, 186.

4. Douglas-Radcliff Umstead, *The Mirror of Our Anguish: A Study of Pirandello's Narrative Writings* (Cranbury, NJ and London, 1978, p. 162.

5. *Ibid.*, pp. 166-167.

6. *Ibid.*, p. 163.

7. Gaspare Giudice, *Luigi Pirandello* (Torino, 1963), p. 179. My translation.

8. *Ibid.*, p. 319: "è una grande diavoleria . . . d'una originalità che grida."

Narrative in Pirandello's Plays

Why did Pirandello, already successful as a writer of fiction, turn to writing plays at the age of fifty? The immediate answer is simple enough: he began to write for the stage, in the dialect of his native Agrigento, Sicily (later "translated" into official Italian by the playwright himself), at the request of the Sicilian actor Angelo Musco, who was looking for new scripts. These early plays, like many later ones, were often drawn from his short stories and retain the realistic setting of their source, but they also carry the seeds of a new kind of theater, an altogether new vision of the stage that emerged fully articulated in 1921 with what has become his best-known and most popular play, the first of the three "theater plays," *Six Characters in Search of an Author.*

With his early Sicilian plays, Pirandello shows an intuitive understanding of the distinct nature of drama, what T. S. Eliot calls "the third voice of poetry,"[1] in which the author is heard through the voices of the autonomous characters he has created and to whom he has allowed full freedom of expression. He must have realized also, although he continued to write short stories and novels, that drama allowed him the kind of experimentation that promised exciting results.

With the international success of *Six Characters,* drama became his top priority; but as early as *Pensaci, Giacomino!* (*Think It Over, Jamie!*) and as late as *Lazzaro* (*Lazarus*), *La Nuova Colonia* (*The New Colony*), and in all three of his "theater plays," Sicilian conventions and settings, the economical and psychological struggles of the poverty-stricken people he knew

---

A brief version of this essay first appeared in PSA, *the annual volume of The Pirandello Society of America, Vol. XIII, 1998. Enlarged and revised.*

all too well, victims of the stifling, closed society of southern Italy — the familiar subjects of his fiction — find their way into the dramatic script.

His fiction sets forth in detail and with great compassion the restrictions of Sicilian life, the mindfulness of death as a living reality, the vital importance of property, and how love and integrity are at the mercy of those two constants that direct and rule the lives of people who are subject to the merciless demands of a barren, hostile environment. Again and again, even in the "theater plays," he presents in some form or other in excruciating detail, the rigorous moral demands of a closed society, entrenched conventions that sacrifice youth and love for marriages of convenience. His fiction is a social-historical tapestry woven in the somber colors of hopeless circumstances.

His plays, often set against the same depressing and barren landscape, give us many of the same characters who, in the distinctive format of drama, are allowed to assert themselves in a new way. This is not altogether surprising: plays have a life of their own, very different from that of fiction. But in Pirandello's plays, another, totally unexpected imperative has taken hold. The oppressive background of his fiction recedes, and the characters, often cut from the same fabric as those of his fiction, are shown seeking a personal certainty that is not always related to their surroundings, we hear them struggling for self-conscious awareness, building as it were the internal landscape where the self resides. The dramatic conflict is focused on the individual's search for identity, on recognizing what is illusory and what is real.

In this connection, certain notions must be dismissed, before we continue. Many critics insist that Pirandello was a relativist and that his common theme is "reality vs. illusion." He had met Einstein and no doubt knew something about the new scientific theory; but nothing in his own writings suggests a relativistic or solipsistic attitude toward the world. Those who believe he is a "relativist" usually refer to his plays, conveniently forgetting his fiction — a dangerous thing for any critic to do. The fact is, in both his fiction and his plays Pirandello upholds the *accessibility of truth*. He reminds us constantly of the movement from consciousness to self-consciousness, the scrutiny that turns simple awareness into recognition of the opposite, the prelude to real answers. Certainty is both a *process* and a *product*, a Socratic spiraling toward knowledge. Accepting facts and events that have not been examined and made part of one's inner life results in the detached skepticism of a Laudisi in *Così è (se vi pare)* *(Right You are! [If You Think So])* Unfortunately, many critics have mistakenly identified Laudisi's efficient questioning of reality with Pirandello's. But Laudisi is not a spokesman for Pirandello, only a voice among many. He is the eternal skeptic, the unresolved double image. For Laudisi the dichotomy of simple consciousness and self-consciousness, the awareness that should lead to recognition and identity, is never resolved — just as the others in that play insist on confusing external "facts" with "truth" and therefore cannot understand the process by which reality is attained, what — at the end of the play — Signora Frola and Ponza are able to assert without contradiction.[2]

It is this process of *definition* that Pirandello assumes as the major burden of his plays. There is nothing tentative about it, nothing relativistic. Perhaps it was the early experience with fiction, the result of his rich descriptions of individuals trapped in a no-win situation, that prompted him to find in drama, after the early plays for Musco, an outlet for the paradoxes inherent in our daily lives, as we strive to know ourselves — what the critic Robert Brustein has described as "the dramatization of the very act of creation." In his words, the plays are Pirandello's "most original achievement," his *dramatis personae* "being both his product and his process."[3] The "theater plays," together with *Così è (se vi pare)* and

Enrico IV, are perhaps the best examples of Pirandello's effort to dramatize that process by depicting character in a moment of crisis, within a spiraling action that circles back on itself toward greater understanding. Statement is replaced by paradoxes and dialectical inversions. The Realistic play has been transformed into a new kind of drama.

Not surprisingly, Pirandello's restructured stage reflects nonetheless much of what he had used so effectively in his fiction, especially narrative. His short play, *L'uomo dal fiore in bocca (The Man With the Flower in His Mouth)* is virtually a long monologue by a dying man, a narrative that could easily have been part of a story or novel, in which the main character relates to a total stranger his feelings, how the cancer has affected his relationship with his wife, etc. In *La patente (The License)*, Chiarchiaro recounts the story of his misery by way of explaining and justifying his seemingly bizarre decision to turn the town's prejudice against him, as a carrier of the "evil eye," into an unusual "official" means of livelihood, by making every effort to lose the court case he has instigated against the authorities and thus be "recognized" as someone to be avoided. The paradox is explained at great length, unanswerable in its bizarre logic. It begins with this poignant account of the conditions which have led up to his strange actions.

> For years I worked hard and honestly. They threw me out, kicked me into the gutter because they said I had the Evil Eye! In the gutter, with my wife a paralytic, bedridden for the last three years, and with two young daughters who, if you could just see them, Your Honor, it would break your heart, they're so pretty, both of them. But no one will have anything to do with them because they're mine.... And do you know what we live on now, all four of us? On the bread my son takes out of his own mouth, and he a family man with three children of his own to feed![4]

In a similar vein, the two main protagonists of *All'uscita (At the Exit)* indulge in detailed reminiscences as they brood about the life they have just left behind. In this passage, The Philosopher describes his dog as a prelude to thoughts about God.

> . . . I used to walk him everywhere. His thin legs would tremble so and his paws would seem to skim over the ground. But he used to drive me to distraction because he'd want to rush into every church we passed. And I'd have to run after him, calling his name: "Bibi, Bibi, here, Bibi!" he could never understand why a nice-looking dog like him wasn't allowed inside a church. When I scolded him, he'd sit up and lift one of his front paws and whimper, one ear cocked, the other flopping down, and he'd look at me as if to say that obviously the place was empty and of course he could go in. "What do you mean it's empty?" I'd say, petting him. "That place contains the highest of human sentiments, Bibi, a sentiment so high that it could not content itself with living only in the hearts of men and had to build itself a house outside, and what a house! With domes, naves, columns, gold, marble, great works of art."[5]

The Fat Man, in turn, tells about the moment of his death and the reaction of his wife and her lover:

> . . . she was so happy as I lay dying that she didn't even try to hide it. Her joy wasn't due so much to my imminent death as to the spectacle of black despair her lover provided as he stood at my bedside, racking his brains to find some way of keeping me alive. . . . He couldn't help but like me. And I assure you that from the very first I felt terribly sorry for this man, because no sooner had she betrayed me than my wife turned on him with all the ferocity and hate she had until then reserved for me. With me she resumed the lightly affectionate, slightly bantering tone of our early courtship, when she'd do such things as stick a flower in my mouth and tell me I looked funny. It wasn't long before I had the satisfaction of knowing for certain that the man who thought he had done me wrong by deceiving me was being put through the same torment I had suffered, and that his agony was complicated further by a cruel and sincere feeling of remorse. For this man, you see, my dying was the greatest of

misfortunes, since through my death my wife hoped to free herself, not so much from me as from him. In a sense, you see, he was only my shadow, not because he was always around me, but because my status of husband provided him with his stature of lover. The kind of a lover a woman takes depends very much on the kind of husband she has. When the body dies, the shadow dies with it. As long as I was around, he could be sure of remaining her lover. But now? With me gone, why limit herself to one? And that one the boring shadow of a body that no longer exists. She'll take another. Perhaps more than one.[6]

Even as The Fat Man goes on to say how the lover will surely kill the woman "to stop her from laughing," she appears, killed indeed by her lover, as her husband had predicted.

In these excerpts, as in the ones that follow, narrative is brought in unobtrusively but always relevant to the action surrounding it. This may seem obvious, but it is not always the case. Narrative introduced in drama is not always sustained successfully: it may prove distracting or, worse, disruptive. It can easily shift the focus and make the reconnection with dialogue difficult, impossible even. But like Shakespeare before him and playwrights like Edward Albee[7] after him, Pirandello proved himself, from the very beginning, an absolute master of dramatic narrative.

It gets even better (it that's possible) in the later, full-length plays. In *Così è (se vi pare)* (*Right You Are! [If You Think So]*). Pirandello reaches a new level of dramatic narrative in Signora Frola's account of how she and her "daughter" are not allowed to meet face to face but must resort to exchanging notes by lowering and raising a basket — and Signor Ponza's contradictory account of the intricate, paradoxical relationship the three have come to accept for themselves. In these narratives, needed to lay out the dilemma at the heart of the play, Ponza, Signora Frola, and the "wife-daughter" come alive in the descriptions of their daily routines, appearances, recalled past events that triggered the strange accommodations they have had to make — narratives of conflicting scenarios, as it were.

But it is in the "theater plays" that Pirandello dramatizes the very *process* of conversion from narrative to drama. We can only guess how he came to see the possibilities of utilizing the stage in this way; but there can be no doubt that he grasped clearly the potential of the idea and deliberately turned to explore it. The first striking example is in *Sei personaggi in cerca d'autore* (*Six Characters in Search of an Author.*) Professional actors are rehearsing in an empty theater. They are interrupted by "real-life" characters looking for an author who will dramatize their story of incest and adultery. The Director finally agrees to work out a tentative script focused on the day when The Father went to Madame Pace's millinery establishment (a front for a brothel) and almost had sex with one of the prostitutes, who happened to be the daughter from his wife's liaison with a man who had been forced on her by her own husband, thinking she would be happier with him. But neither The Father nor The Step-Daughter are satisfied with the efforts of the actors. They, the "real-life" characters, keep interrupting, insisting finally that only they can play out the story, since they have actually *lived* it.

The story itself is narrated in bits and pieces in the latter part of the first act: The Father's taking care of the expanded family after the death of the man to whom he had entrusted his wife and who had turned out to be a much better companion for her, giving her three more children during their years together; The Mother's agonized response to the rejection by The Son, her only legitimate offspring, The Step-Daughter's bitterness toward The Father, who had decided The Mother needed another kind of man and who, even after sending her away, would often go by The Step-Daughter's school to watch her, as came out of the building, on her way home:

I used to see him waiting outside the school for me to come out. He came to see how I was growing up.[8]

The Father himself takes pains to recount at length the strange longing that drew him back to the family he had sent away, especially its new members, who were created by him (as he tells it) by his *will*, his decision to send off his wife with another man, who was more suited for her. This is a small segment of that account:

> After she [indicating The Mother] went away, my house seemed suddenly empty. She was my incubus, but she filled my house. I was like a dazed fly alone in the empty rooms. This boy here [indicating The Son] was educated *away* from home, and when he came back, he seemed to me no more mine. With his mother to stand between him and me, he grew up entirely for himself, on his own, apart, with no tie of intellect or affection binding him to me. And then — strangely but true — I was driven, by curiosity at first and then by some tender sentiment, towards her family, which had come into being through my will. The thought of her began gradually to fill up the emptiness I felt all around me. I wanted to know if she was happy in living out the simple daily duties of life. I wanted to think of her as fortunate and happy because far away from the complicated torments of my spirit. And so, to have proof of this, I used to watch that child coming out of school.[9]

In this way we learn of the years during which The Father lost track of his family, how he finally found them again, his feelings toward them.

> I couldn't possibly know that after the death of that man, they had decided to return here, that they were in misery, and that she [pointing to The Mother] had gone to work as a modiste at a shop of the type of that of Madame Pace.[10]

At one point in this narrative, Pirandello has The Manager express an obvious concern, one no doubt shared by the audience:

> A bit discursive this, you know![11]

The Italian underscores our argument more clearly:

> Ma tutto questo è racconto, signori miei! [But, my dear sirs, all this is narrative!]

To which The Son answers contemptuously:

> Ma sì, letteratura! letteratura! [But of course! literature! literature!]

And The Father responds:

> Ma che letteratura! Questa è vita, signore! Passione! [What literature! This is life, Sir! Passion!]

And The Capocomico reminds them:

> Sarà! Ma irrapresentabile! [That might be! But it can't be staged!][12]

Obviously the narrative is necessary to highlight the sea-change about to take place, the transformation of an involved, splintered story into the immediacy of drama. The part of the story that is turned by The Manager and The Father into a rough script during the first break focuses on the meeting between The Father and The Step-Daughter in Madame Pace's establishment, a scene that is extremely distressing for all concerned and certainly is meant to be the climax of the projected play. We already know that on her return, after her companion's death, The Mother found much-needed employment as a *modiste* in Madame Pace's establishment, never suspecting that behind the façade of a milliner's boutique, the woman ran a brothel and that she had hired the Mother to have access to The Step-Daughter, who, because of their desperate need for money, accepts the offer to "entertain" Madame Pace's male clients. The scripted scene of the aborted sexual encounter is enacted *twice*: by the professional actors (constantly interrupted by the "real-life" protagonists, who have nothing but criticism for the actors), then by The Father and Step-Daughter, playing themselves — another set of "masks" in this extraordinary layering of roles. Neither one had been aware of the relationship that exists between them, until The Mother, coming upon them by chance, brings the truth to light.

The effort to dramatize the story of what in those days would have been interpreted as an incestuous sexual encounter is followed by an enactment, by the "real'life" characters, of the seemingly accidental drowning of the little girl, in a fountain, and the discovery of the young boy hiding nearby, holding a gun, which he turns on himself as the others watch in horror. The acting group takes this to be really happening, and of course it is happening, as a "replay"; the children's deaths — like everything else we have been seeing and hearing — have already taken place. This is the obsessive drama the six "characters" are burdened with, the baggage they carry with them, to be enacted over and over again, without resolution or absolution. After this last scene, the six intruders leave as suddenly as they had appeared, no doubt to seek another place, another author. The "professional" actors go back to rehearsing their play, which happens to be Pirandello's *Il gioco delle parti (The Rules of the Game)*. We've come full circle.

Throughout, the uncompromising directions of the "real-life" characters as they attempt to turn their narrative into drama point to an effort at communication that is doomed to failure. In their eyes, the "professional" actors will never be able to take on successfully the roles assigned them, since they have not "lived" the events described to them. Like the curious neighbors in *Così è (se vi pare)*, the certainty of the six "characters" is beyond them.

In *Ciascuno a suo modo (Each In His Own Way)*, the second of the "theater plays," we have *two* abortive plays: the play on stage and the action "off stage" in the lobby of the theater — all part of the script, of course; all taking place on the actual stage. The directions call for a pre-performance action outside the theater, where newspaper vendors are advertising a special edition of *Corriere della sera*, in which a recent scandal is rehashed, the very story dramatized by

Pirandello in the play being shown that evening.

Briefly, the sordid story is about a a promising young sculptor, Giacomo La Vela, who was engaged to a well-known actress, Amelia Moreno, and committed suicide a month earlier, when he found his fiancée *in flagrante* with a prominent citizen, Baron Nuti. This "prelude" to the play continues in the lobby of the theater, where friends unsuccessfully try to dissuade Moreno from staying for the play in which she is featured. In another part of the lobby, Baron Nuti's friends are also trying to get him to leave but he assures them he only wants to see if Moreno will show up: he needs to see her. The two groups join the rest of the crowd now entering the theater, as the play is about to begin.

When the curtain comes down for the break at the end of Act One it is immediately raised again, showing a replica of the lobby and people coming into it for the intermission. In this first *Intermezzo corale*, we hear several critics argue about the merits and weaknesses of the play they have been watching. When the gong sounds for Act Two, three of the critics stay behind to watch as Moreno is restrained by her friends from going back "inside" to attack the actors on stage — no doubt to insist on *her* version of the "story" being dramatized, in much the same way as The Father and The Step-Daughter tried to do in *Six Characters*. This "intermission" ends with Moreno and her friends returning to their seats to watch the rest of the play.

At the end of the second act, the curtain is lowered and, once again, raised immediately, as before. In this second *Intermezzo corale* we are again in the lobby of the theater. There is a huge commotion, a lot of yelling and shouting off stage (meant to be coming from inside the theater, where, in fact all is quiet as the audience sits and watches all this). Moreno has apparently managed to gain the stage and has slapped the leading lady playing the part of Moreno — or was it the author she slapped? (someone asks). In the midst of this chaos, the Director, several actors, and other theater personnel appear, wondering what else to expect. What happens is that, in spite of the efforts of friends to keep them apart, Moreno and Nuti suddenly come face to face. They quarrel. Nuti manages to steer her clear of the crowd that has gathered and quickly leads her away. By now the actors, thoroughly frustrated and angry have also left. The curtain finally comes down, and a member of the troupe appears in front of it to announce that the unfortunate incidents they have witnessed make it impossible to continue. There will be no third act.

The ending is as abrupt and disruptive as the one in *Six Characters* and as the one in the third of the "theater plays," *Questa sera si recita a soggetto*[13] (*Tonight We Improvise*). This last of the "theater plays" has other features which make it stand apart in a special way, not the least of which is the large paradox evident from the start: it is advertised as an "improvisation" but it is, in fact, a carefully scripted play, meant to be repeated exactly as set down by its author.

As in the earlier two plays, the audience is part of the pyramid layering of the script — much more open and deliberate here than in the other two plays. Il Dottor Hinkfuss, cast as the Director (not the director of the play itself) has come into the theater from a side door to climb the three steps to the stage from one side. The footlights have gone on but are not raised to full power; the gong announcing the raising of the curtain has not sounded. From behind the closed curtain, voices are raised in protest, a quarrel among the actors. Hinkfuss has gone to stand in front of the curtain. The spectators, impatient and restless for the play to begin, toss questions at him (naturally all of this part of the script but giving the impression of an impromptu exchange); but instead of explaining the delay in starting, or what the racket backstage is all about, Hinkfuss talks about his choice for the program.

It's a short story by Pirandello; he tells them; but relax: no danger of anything happening here like what happened with the other two plays, where the directors saw their work end in disruption and chaos. He won't let that happen here! Pirandello's name doesn't appear even on the posters ("il suo nome non figura nemmeno sui manifesti"). I've gotten rid of him" ("L'ho eliminato"). His explanation takes us to still another level in this large paradox about the nature of theater and dramatic art:

> Ho preso una sua novella, come avrei potuto prendere quella d'un altro. Ho preferito una sua perchè tra tutti gli scrittori di teatro è forse il solo che abbia mostrato di comprendere che l'opera dello scrittore è finito nel punto stesso ch'egli ha finito di scrivere l'ultima parola. Risponderà di questa sua opera al pubblico dei lettori e alla critica letteraria. Non può ne deve rispondere al pubblico degli spettatori e ai signori critici drammatici, che giudicano sedendo in teatro.
>
> (I took one of his short stories, as I might have taken one by another. I preferred one of his because, of all the writers for the theater, he's probably the only one who has ever shown he understands that the task of the writer ends at the very moment he puts down the last word. He will answer for this work of his to the public, the readers out there, and to literary criticism. He cannot and should not answer to the audience and drama critics, the gentlemen who judge while sitting in the theater.)

And in answer to (scripted) objections coming from the audience, he responds:

> No signori. Perché in teatro l'opera dello scrittore non c'è piú.
>
> (No, my friends. Because in the theater the writer's work is not there any more.)

And when someone asks: "So what's there, then?" Hinkfuss replies:

> La creazione scenica che n'avrò fatta io, e che è soltanto mia. (230)

(The stage creation that I will have made it into and which is mine alone.)

What follows is a virtual monologue of almost three dense pages, in which Hinkfuss explains the nature of the transformation that must take place, that someone like him must effect, if narrative is to come alive on the stage, not just once, not just here, but in other venues, with other actors, on other occasions. Hinkfuss assures everyone they will indeed be entertained by what he has done with Pirandello's story. This long prelude ends with Hinkfuss calling for the gong to be sounded.

The curtain rises; but instead of the play, we have still another brief prelude in front of a thin inner curtain with an opening in the center: Hinkfuss wants to introduce the actors. He begins with the Leading Man, who refuses to appear at first. When he does come forward, it is to protest at being introduced by his own name, given the fact that he is there as Rico Verri, in full military garb, to improvise, according to Hinfuss's instructions, another man's life. He is ready to do that and will come out again only when it's time to play his part. With that, he retreats behind the inner curtain. Hinkfuss (now embarrassed) has yet to absorb the argument about the distinction between the role and the character, the assumed identity and the real-life identity of the actor. The Leading Man comes out to explain more fully:

> Lei deve credere soltanto che qua, sotto questi panni, il signor . . . (*dirà il suo nome*) non c'è' piú; perché impegnatosi con lei a recitare questa sera a soggetto, per aver pronte le parole che debbone nascere, nascere dal personaggio che rappresento, e spontanea l'azione, e naturale ogni gesto; il signor . . . (*c. s.*) deve vivere il personaggio di *Rico Verri*, essere *Rico Verri*: ed è, è già; tanto che, come le dicevo in principio, non so se potrà adattarsi a tutte le combinazioni e sorprese e giochetti di luce e d'ombra preparati da lei per divertire il pubblico. Ha capito? (238)

(You have to believe only that here, under these clothes, Mister (*gives his name*) is no longer there; because having agreed with you to improvise tonight, to be ready with the words that must rise, rise out of the character I represent, and the action spontaneous, and every gesture natural, Mister _____ (*as above*) must live the character of *Rico Verri*, be *Rico Verri*; and he is, he already is that, so much so that, as I said at the beginning, I don't know if he will be able to adjust to all the combinations and surprises, and little tricks of light and shadows, you've worked out to entertain the public. Do you understand?)

This exchange comes to an end as a loud slap resounds behind the curtain. Several new voices are raised in protest, a new quarrel flares up among the actors. Hinkfuss himself doesn't know what's going on, until one by one, the actors come forward, bringing their quarrel with them (and indirectly introducing themselves to the audience).

The idea of "improvisation" apparently has inspired one of them to introduce something that is unacceptable to the actor at the receiving end. The actor who has been slapped by the woman who will be playing the role of Signora Ignazia is not at all happy with her "improvisation" (among other complaints he puts forward: her slap will smear his make-up). Hinkfuss tries to re-establish some kind of order, reminding them that they are quarreling in full view of the audience. This goes on a while longer, until the actress who had delivered the slap reminds Hinkfuss that most of them have now been introduced to the audience. The remaining four women are called out and bow to the audience as they too are introduced. Their entrance leads smoothly into the core action — the extraordinary argument about the layering of characters and roles, story and play, script and improvisation, life and the illusion of the theater, temporarily put aside, to be resumed at the very end.

Or so it seems. Hinkfuss takes time to remind the audience that all they have seen and heard is part of the "improvisation" and orders the woman playing Signora Ignazia to proceed. She looks confused: what is she supposed to do next? Continue, as we agreed, Hinkfuss says. But there *was* no agreement, she insists. In the end, she calls out the others and they arrange themselves on stage (not without some bickering about the instructions Signora Ignazia is giving them).

Have we begun at last? The Leading Lady, comes out of her role as the abused young wife, Mommina, to assert that she will not tolerate the arbitrary capers others may wish to indulge, having been given license to "improvise." She has taken her instructions seriously and has prepared her part within the outline provided by Hinkfuss. New quarrels threaten to erupt, but Hinkfuss manages to defuse the latent jealousies and objections, reminding them that he is directing and that they must follow his instructions. The curtain comes down on what we suddenly realize was the first act of the play.

I have gone into some detail to underscore the unique format of this third "theater play" — paradoxically, a scripted "improvisation" based on a story, which moves in and out of the illusion of the stage, which moves characters in and out of their roles, which uses the audience as part of the cast — because, in addition to expanding what was already done in the earlier two plays, it also provides the most direct articulation of the metamorphosis itself of narrative into drama. Pirandello's argument about his new vision of the stage is dramatized, as it were, in a play that appears to be a *prelude* to a play, one that is full of paradoxes and contradictions that somehow do not cancel out but add to the spiraling toward some kind of truth. All this may seem strange at first, but it is also riveting. We are drawn into the experience of a kaleidoscopic, many-faceted stage, a telescopic view in which we constantly shift from the reality of immediate experience to the distance of illusions that are meant to be real.

There is nothing tentative about this extraordinary play, in which the very process of dramatizing a narrative, converting a story (real or imagined) into drama, is also *explained*. It is a process that intrigued playwrights who followed Pirandello; but none of them succeeded so well and in so many different ways. But we're not through yet. In the second act we are led into the "improvisation," which the actors still have difficulty accepting and persist in questioning, from time to time. Their occasional interruptions do not seriously impair the action, which now moves forward with comparative ease.

Signoria Ignazia and her four daughters, in colorful evening dress, are on their way to the theater, escorted by five officers, aviators, part of a unit stationed in town. They too are dressed for the evening in elegant uniforms. They pass the Cabaret, where Signora Ignazia's husband Sampognetta, the father of the four pretty girls, has gone to admire La Chanteuse, a blues singer who weeps every time she sings. A quiet man, dominated by his wife, Sampognetta is mesmerized by the woman who seems to have gone through some heart-breaking experience and responds to her pain with tears of his own. All this is a big joke for the boisterous young men of the town, who see in poor Sampognetta an infatuated old man. Looking for excitement, one of the merrymakers picks up a program and cuts out two paper horns — the universal symbol of the "cuckold" — which he then places quietly on top of Sampognetta's hat. There is laughter all around; even Sampognetta joins in, not knowing why they are laughing. When he leaves the Cabaret and runs into his wife and daughters on their way to the theater, he is quickly made aware of the nasty trick played on him. He curses the young men, who are enjoying all this. The young women try to soothe their father; Signora Ignazia calls him an imbecile, an easy target for all the louts hanging around. The officers stand up for the women, insults are exchanged, but the women soon continue on their way to the theater, after Signora Ignazia dismisses her husband, ordering him to go home. Verri is the only one of the officers escorting the women who insists on taking the matter seriously, as though he too has been insulted.

Hinkfuss, all but forgotten in this exchange of harsh words, suddenly comes running up to congratulate them on the execution of the scene, calls for the next one to begin, and returns to his seat in the orchestra. An old Italian melodrama is being projected on a bare white wall which serves as a large screen. The women and their escorts, coming in late, make a noisy entrance and fuss about the seating arrangements, creating a disturbance. People around them call for silence. The women toss back unflattering comments. Hinkfuss gets up and tells the actors to quiet down, not to overdo it, but the bickering persists.

Verri, uncomfortable throughout, is ready to leave; so is Signora Ignazia, who resents having been insulted for coming in late. She storms out, the others behind her as the episode ends. In the silence that follows, Hinkfuss jumps on stage and explains that those who wish to spend the intermission in the lobby can do so but urges a few to remain in their seats and watch as he transforms the stage for the next scene.

The play now continues into the lobby, where Signora Ignazia's group (mingling with the real audience) separates into twos and threes, drifting in different directions, seeking refreshments and keeping up a scattered dialogue. At the end of this first intermission, in which the actors have continued to "perform," people start coming back to their seats. Hinkfuss is still on the open stage, where he has been supervising the setting up of the next scene, an airfield (obviously programmed for the benefit of the aviator-officers). To study the effect he has created, Hinkfuss goes down into the orchestra, where he stands in the aisle to survey his creation. After a few minutes, he climbs back on stage and shouts for the lights to be put out and the entire set to be removed. In the darkness, the curtain is lowered, to allow the production crew to remove the set. Hinkfuss, now standing in front of the closed curtain, quickly orders the lights on again, to make sure the audience have settled in their seats again, giving time also to Signora Ignazia and her daughters to reach "home," that is, to continue with the next scene (the one on the airfield now deleted).

The scene is Sampognetta's house, where the party continues. Sampognetta obviously has returned to the Cabaret, instead of following his wife's orders to stay indoors. It is after midnight, but Signora Ignazia seems unwilling to bring the evening to a close, even though she is suffering a terrible toothache. Verri goes in search of an all-night pharmacy where he can get something to relieve her pain. She is truly suffering, but part of her restlessness, we have come to understand, must be attributed to her unhappiness at finding herself stranded in a small town with four pretty daughters and no improvement in sight. A native of Naples, she still longs for the big city, flaunting "continental" airs, ignoring the stifling local conventions by entertaining after midnight, inviting strangers into her home, dressing herself and her four daughters in colorful gowns that are out of place in a small town, almost deliberately, it would seem, to encourage gossip. Unhappy at having been forced to live in such a place, at the mercy of rude country bumpkins, she vents her impatience and frustration on those around her: a domineering superiority toward her husband, who apparently has gotten used to it; a devil-may-care attitude toward the local conventions and traditions in which a woman must not dress or act as she does and certainly not go gallivanting around after midnight in the company of strangers. Her restlessness is interpreted by others as a lack of propriety and discretion. All this makes her an easy target for gossip in the small town.

Trying to ease their mother's discomfort while waiting for Verri to return, the girls are encouraged to sing and dance; Mommina reluctantly joins in. It soon becomes clear that Verri's interest in Mommina is more than a passing one; he is overly protective and not at all pleased when he returns to find her singing, decked out in a costume her sisters have put together. He accuses his colleagues of having fun at his expense and attacks them. They fight back. Signora Ignazia orders him to leave her house. He refuses, counting on some kind of understanding between him and Mommina. His intentions, he makes clear, unlike those of his colleagues, are "honest" and above board. He doesn't want Mommina to be the subject of gossip, her reputation tarnished in any way. Still, his rage at finding her entertaining the group seems excessive. His colleagues attribute his black mood to his "bad Sicilian blood."

In the midst of this intense drama of violence and jealousy, the Leading Man playing Verri comes out of his role to scold the Leading Lady playing Mommina for filtering unexpected phrases into the "improvised" dialogue and forcing them into a new direction. There is some disputing about this; Hinkfuss interrupts, assuring them that everything is moving along fine and urges them to continue.

This little scene is interrupted by a loud pounding on the outside door. The actors, in a tiff for having their strategies destroyed by the Leading Lady's unexpected insertion, still angry with her for the interruption, ignore the cue announcing the next scene. Instead of answering the door, they stand around bickering, until the actor playing Sampognetta appears, all bloodied, he too outside his role, impatient as to why no one has come to open the door, the signal for his big dying speech. Once again, Hinkfuss forces them back into their roles. La Chanteuse and others try to hold on to Sampognetta as he falls, mortally wounded, having been stabbed in the Cabaret by La Chanteuse's jealous lover.

The women cluster around him, someone calls for a doctor, but no one moves, waiting for Sampognetta to deliver his dying speech. Instead he just smiles up at them. Finally, he stands up, out of character again, and tells Hinkfuss that he can't find anything to say, since his big entrance was spoiled. He is indignant at having been denied the opportunity of a dramatic entrance followed by a big dying speech (summarizing its contents, in effect, as he rants on). The others move close again to hold him up, but he simply slides to the floor again, as though dead. His "daughters" begin to cry in earnest. Hinkfuss shouts his approval, calls for the lights to be dimmed on stage, orders everybody off, and gives directions for the next scene. Mommina reminds him the women have to change into black mourning dresses. To give them time to change, he orders the curtain to be lowered and the lights on. Standing before the closed curtain, he now addresses the audience at some length (allowing the production crew to set up the next segment), assuring them that Scampognetta's moving entrance, omitted tonight because of the unfortunate mix-up on stage, would certainly be enacted tomorrow, The scene is his creation, he takes pain to point out; it is not in the original story. Pirandello would have shied away from all that blood and passion (he tells them); if he had wanted to kill Scampagnetta, he would probably have shown him dying of a heart attack or a stroke. But (he goes on) you see how much better my version is: he has got to die, one way of the other, thus plunging the family into dire poverty, providing the motivation for Mommina's brash decision to marry Verri, whose father is known for his fierce jealousy.

> Come non si figura questa benedetta ragazza la sorte che l'attende? i patti, i patti a cui Rico Verri, sposandola per la picca di spuntarla contro quei suoi compagni ufficiali, si sarà arreso con quel padre geloso e usurajo, e quali altri patti avrà con sé stesso stabiliti, non solo per compensarci del sacrificio che gli costa quel puntiglio, ma anche per rialzarsi di fronte ai suoi compaesani a cui é ben nota la fama che gode la famiglia della moglie? Chi sa come le farà scontare i piaceri che ha potuto darle la vita come finora l'ha vissuta in casa, con la sua mamma e le sue sorelle? Persuasioni, come vedete, validissime. . . . Il Verri farà

per lei, non uno, ma tre duelli con quegli ufficiali che subito, al primo colpo della sventura, si sono tutti squagliati: la passione dei melodrammi, in fondo, ce l'ha anche lei in comune con le sorelle. (289)

(Why can't this blessed girl see what's in store for her? the reasons, the reasons why Rico Verri marrying her to win points over his fellow-officers, and for other reasons he put forward to suit himself, went along with that jealous usurer father of his not only to justify the sacrifice that whim cost him but also to regain his standing among the townspeople, who know all too well the kind of reputation his wife's family enjoys? Who knows how he'll make her pay for the good times at home, until now, with her mother and sisters? Sound reasoning, as you see, perfectly logical. . . . Verri will fight for her not one but three duels with those officers who, at the first sign of trouble, stole away; actually, she too [Mommina], like her sisters, has a passion for melodrama.)

He has been filling time, waiting for the scene to be set up, but he's also been giving us the narrative behind the drama. Now, impatient to start again, he asks what's holding things up. The actors all march out to complain that they can't go on with an improvisation that allows for the deletion of scenes, arbitrary insertions that destroy the continuity and sequence agreed on. They announce that they will march off, refuse to continue, unless Hinkfuss leaves instead.

The stagehands and all the others involved in the production, have come out to watch the quarrel. The actors accuse one another of this and that, all of them turning, finally, on Hinkfuss, who is literally pushed off the stage, protesting loudly. The actors now take over, still out of their roles, and sketch out the plan for the next scene. Mommina is made up by the other actresses to look the part of the long-suffering, spent wife, unable to extricate herself from a terrible marriage. When they are satisfied with her make-up, the women move quietly into the dark wings, leaving

The Leading Lady alone on stage. The play is about to pick up again.

Back in her role as Mommina, The Leading Lady bangs on the walls, muttering like a madwoman. From the wings the actress playing Signora Ignazia reads, as though from a book, the conditions in which Verri has kept his wife a virtual prisoner, doors and windows all locked during the day, allowing her some fresh air at an open window only late at night.

The narrative from the wings ends with the appearance of Rico Verri. By now, his position and disposition have been clarified: he has become a victim of his own obsessive jealousy, unable to dismiss suspicions, even with Mommina locked up all day. His senseless jealousy wants to reach down into her mind and soul, wants to know what she's thinking, even what she dreams when asleep. Even the bits of songs the poor woman brings up from time to time, from the tortured depths of her being, are snatched away by Verri's violent rage, his all-consuming despair.

From the dark wings, the women talk to Mommina, insult Verri, who in turn accuses them of having sold themselves and accuses his wife of having allowed other men to embrace her, to kiss her. In his furious rage, he kisses, bites her, tears at her hair. Mommina cries out in desperation and her two little girls, frightened, come running in. Verri storms out. Exhausted from the trauma she has just endured, Mommina hugs her little girls and tries to comfort them. As though on cue, the other women slowly emerge from the darkness, their colorful gowns a vivid contrast against the squalid surroundings in which Mommina is trapped. They've come with Totina, now a famous opera star, who will be singing in *Il Trovatore* that night, at the town theater. A copy of the program, found in the overcoat her husband has left behind, brings Mommina out of her weary trance; she is overjoyed to find her sister's name in large letters on the program. The others slip back into the darkness while Mommina tells the little girls about the opera, about their aunt Totina, whom they have never met, who will be singing tonight. She sings some of the familiar arias for her daughters; then seating the little girls, she describes the theater, growing more and more animated as she goes on, until, overcome with the intensity of the effort, she almost collapses. Near total exhaustion, she goes on anyway, describing the red plush curtain with its golden fringes, the women decked out in rich gowns and jewels, the men in their their formal evening attire, slipping now and then into a few lines of remembered arias, reaching back finally to that fateful night when her father was killed and her fate sealed. After one final burst of song, she falls, in a faint. The two little girls, thinking it is all part of what their mother has been acting out for them, remain very still in their seats, as though expecting more.

After a long, painful silence, the voices of the women and Verri reach us. They have heard Mommina singing and have come back to tell her of Totina's great success. They appear at the threshold of the room and stare in amazement at what they find.

From the back of the orchestra, Hinkfuss runs down the aisle to the stage, shouting:

Magnifico! Magnifico quadro! Avete fatto come dicevo io! Questo, nella novella, non c'è! (310)

(Splendid! Splendid! You did what I asked. This is not in the story!)

Mommina is still lying on the floor and the actors now cluster around her, wondering, out of their roles again, if she's really ill. She comes around, as they try to revive her, panting and gasping for breath. The older actor (Scampognetta) complains that this is not what they've been trained to do; or are supposed to do. They shouldn't have to put themselves at risk like this, while acting every night.

Non pretenderà mica che ogni sera uno di noi ci lasci la pelle!

(You're not suggesting, I hope, that every night one of us should risk his life?)

The Leading Man calls for an author. Hinkfuss objects, although he concedes that a script that will allow them to give life again to the characters they have created can be produced for subsequence performances —

> senza piú le impertinenze di questa sera, che il pubblico ci vorrà perdonare. (311)

(without any of the outrageous liberties taken this evening, which I hope the audience will excuse.)

There is no other play quite like *Questa sera si recita a soggetto*. Albee's *Fragments* and *Box and Quotations from Chairman Mao* approximate it in the effort to clear the stage and especially in the effective use of narrative. The dizzying pyrotechnics of a play in the making, an improvisation that cannot survive without a script, the constant shifting from narrative to drama, is a stunning "experiment," fully realized, yet to be matched. Not only does it present us with a fragmented play on a new kind of stage, it also raises intriguing questions about the actor and his role, the role and the mask, the character and his relation to the text, the director's relation to the actors and the audience, the place of a script in the production of a play, etc. The nature of drama, the idea of the play itself comes under scrutiny. It is a fitting conclusion to the "theater plays."

It would be rewarding in this context to explore *Enrico IV* (*Henry IV*) — the play in which "intruders" find their ideal author and where narrative and drama are perfectly fused, as it were, in a multi-layering of time, place, and roles. Let me suggest this much at least: the eleventh-century setting in which we watch the Eisensteinian superimposition of masks and identities is the most memorable conversion to drama of a narrative itself on two levels. On one level, we have the "mad" emperor's historical account of the events dealing with the Countess Matelda of Tuscany and the excommunicated then later penitent Emperor Henry IV; on a second level, we have the reconstructed story of the carneval pageant in which, twenty years earlier, the protagonist was pushed from his horse and lost his memory. In superimposing these two stories from widely-separated moments in the past on to an immediate, dramatic present, Pirandello is not only declaring his personal commitment to the new stage he has created but also giving us a brilliant resolution to his "theater plays" and, in so doing, asserting his ingenuity as a playwright.

NOTES

1. T. S. Eliot, "The Three Voices of Poetry," *On Poetry and Poets* (Noonday Press, New York, 1943, etc.,), pp. 96-112.

2. See Luigi Pirandello, *Maschere Nude* 2 Vols. (Arnoldo Mondadori Editore, Verona, Italy, 1965), *Così è (se vi pare)* Vol. 1, pp. 1027-1100. See also: *Right You Are (If You Think You Are)*, translated by Stanley Appelbaum (Dover Publications, Mineola, New York, 1997), and Eric Bentley, *It is So (If You Think So)* in *Naked Masks* (E. P. Dutton, New York, 1952), pp. 61-138.

3. "Pirandello's Drama of Revolt," in Glauco Cambon, ed., *Pirandello: A Collection of Critical Essays*, p. 133. See also, Anne Paolucci, *Pirandello's Theater: The Recovery of the Modern Stage for Dramatic Art* (Southern Illinois University Press, Carbondale, 1974; rptd Griffon House Publications, Smyrna DE, 2002).

4. *Pirandello's One-Act Plays*, trans. By William Murray (Samuel French, New York, 1970), p. 135.

5. *Ibid.*, pp. 179-180.

6. *Ibid.*, pp. 183-184.

7. See, for example, Albee's long allegorically suggestive narrative about the dog in *The Zoo Story* (revised recently into a full-length play. *At Home at the Zoo*) and the strange story about the cat in *A Delicate Balance*, etc.

8. Bentley, *It is So (If You Think So)*, p. 227. See also, *Sei personaggi in cerca di un autore*, in *Maschere Nude,*)Vol. I, pp. 69-138.

9. Bentley, *op. cit..* 227-228.

10. *Ibid.*, p. 230.

11. *Ibid.*, p. 228.

12. *Maschere Nude* 2 Vols. (Arnoldo Mondadori Editore, Verona, Italy, 1965), *Sei personnaggi in cerca d'autore*, Vol. 1, pp. 91. (Translations in brackets are my own.)

13. *Maschere Nude, Questa sera si recita a soggetto*, Vol. 1, pp. 221-312. (My translations.)

The New Humor

The temptation will always be strong, for anyone dealing with Pirandello's comedy, to begin with an examination of his little book on humor, *L'Umorismo*.[1] I have tried to resist that temptation for good reason. Pirandello's little treatise has been carefully examined by experts like Professor Dante della Terza, whose incisive essay, "On Pirandello's Humor,"[2] has proved invaluable to most of us interested in the subject, and Professor Antonio Illiano, whose translation of Pirandello's little book (with Daniel P. Testa) supplies indispensable notes as well as a fine introduction. There is also Benedetto Croce's criticism of *L'Umorismo*, as well as the debate over Tilgher's influence on Pirandello and the playwright's response to that debate — all of which take us into a theoretical/philosophical area. My interest is and always has been the plays themselves, and my interest in *L'Umorismo* is triggered by what it tells me about Pirandello's new approach to the theater with regard to comedy and humor. Moreover, in writing his little treatise, Pirandello was not posing as a critical philosopher but explaining with care and conviction an important idea bearing directly on his work, the genial paradox on which his new theater rests: that humor is not always meant to be just funny (as it certainly is at certain moments in *La giarra* [*The Jar*], or in *La patente* [*The License*]); that even when we laugh *at* situations and people our laughter ricochets to sputter and die in the awareness that we are witnessing our own flaws, our own excesses, our own vulnerability. At those moments, paradoxically, humor becomes something close to pathos.

His plays, in fact, force us to reconsider many things that are taken for granted, to turn the obvious into an unknown quantity to be scrutinized and evaluated before it can be accepted as part of our conscious world. In that paradoxical format, all things must be redefined. Della Terza argues that the definition Pirandello gives of *humorism* indicates a dilemma at the core of his aesthetic convictions," that his *feeling of the opposite* is not a feeling at all, "since its activity is overwhelmingly critical, analytical, and rational. By trying to give another name to a cognitive activity, Pirandello, instead of making his dilemma inconspicuous, as he would have liked, ends up by giving the limelight, unwittingly but revealingly, to an all-encompassing and proliferating imagery suggested by the intrusive concept of reflection."[3]

I doubt Pirandello wanted "his dilemma" to remain "inconspicuous"; nor was his approach a philosophical one or a rigorous historical overview, as is the case with his brilliant "Introduzione al teatro italiano"[4] ("Introduction to the Italian Theater"), but an elucidation of something which he considers vital in his new kind of play. His approach is descriptive and easy enough to grasp. He tells us to look at comedy (as used in his plays, obviously) as something other than what it seems, to hold back laughter, to close the distance created by something grotesque, bizarre, unusual or unexpected which ordinarily we would want to steer clear of, with which we do not wish to be associated, and to look at the situation from another perspective. What we then experience is humor that *connects* us to the source, the paradox (or dilemma) of comedy turned into pathos.

By the same token, I have not ignored altogether the philosophical implications of his argument and have welcomed, in fact, some of the more striking statements made by other authors that shed light on that argument. In one case, I was struck by the closing paragraph in Olga Wsster Russell's *Humor in Pascal* (that most paradoxical of all modern thinkers, where in summarizing the "density of techniques" of what the author pointedly calls the "comic humor" of Pascal (to distinguish it from other kinds of humor and other uses of the comic) the author supplies us with a long list of distinctions that may be drawn in analyzing the effects of a paradoxical approach to what were for

Pascal (as for Pirandello) the "shows of life." The main techniques of comic humor bring to focus, the author writes,

> the unexpected within a sentence, or in a situation, or in a figure of speech; the grotesque, the incongruous; caricature by gesture; belittling humor, irony in an adjective, or an adverb, or a verb (in the midst of an otherwise straightforward, serious sentence); irony through disproportion, or by metaphor within metaphor; dynamic and comic antithesis of the small cause and the vast result; the use of derogatory terms or names bringing characters to life in conversation; juxtaposition of the concrete and the abstract, forcing the reader to smile in the obvious attitude of common sense; onomatopoeia as effective as gesture seen on the stage; imagery, concrete and vivid, to point at unreasonableness and foolishness; true comic situations and characters, as in charlatanry in medicine; dramatic situation and crescendo in effect to light up the ridiculous (so close to the sublime); traditional comic themes, *le dupeur dupé*, raised to symbolic meaning; costume as symbol; and the tones of light raillery, teasing, gently irony, sarcasm, bitter and violent satire.

The "humorous effects" of these techniques, the author tells us, are "effective for being presented courteously and charitably, in that Pascal shares with all men the burden of human foolishness."[5]

Pirandello makes similar observations in his discussion on humor, citing in this context Francesco De Sanctis' comment about Machiavelli's "tolerance that understands and absolves"[6] and noting how the author of *Don Quixote* makes it difficult for us actually to laugh at his hero, by troubling us with feelings not only of pity but "even, indeed, of admiration."[7] Yet, I think it is fair to say that Pirandello applies his comic art with an exhaustive thoroughness (at least in his major plays) that is not found in a Pascal or a Cervantes. In the closing pages of *L'Umorismo*, it is the destructive or decompositional thoroughness of his *sentimento del contrario* that is emphasized. Where another artist, an epic or dramatic poet will compose a character from opposite and contrasting elements, the true humorist will do "just the opposite: he will decompose the character into his elements." The true humorist applies a conditional "if," which is but a minute particle of doubt, to begin with — but it is a "minute particle which can be pinned to, and inserted like a wedge into, all events." Inserting that wedge, hammering it into the seemingly solid substance of his subject everywhere, Pirandello tells us, the true humorist literally decomposes what ordinary art composes —

> all that is disorganized, unraveled and whimsical, all the digressions which can be seen in the works of humor, as opposed to the ordered construction, the *composition* of the works of art in general."[8]

That surely is the effect of the *sentimento del contrario* as we find it in Pirandello's plays. We find it as early as 1916, in *Liolà*, a play which in many ways is a romaticized version of Machiavelli's *Mandragola*, (which Pirandello knew well).[9] In it, Uncle Simone, a wealthy old widower, refuses to believe he is impotent, even though his first wife never produced children. Desperate for the heir his new wife Mita, a poor but healthy village girl, can't give him, he makes a deal with a distant cousin, a young woman named Tuzza, who volunteers to give him, when born, her child by Liolà, for Uncle Simone to claim as *his*. Liolà, Mita's equally poor childhood sweetheart, with a reputation as the town "stud," has always kept his love for Mita secret and chaste, knowing there was no future for them together; but when he hears about the "deal" that Tuzza and her mother have made with Uncle Simone, he devises his own counter-plot to make Mita produce the needed heir. He tells her bluntly that she must give her husband what he so desperately wants, if she is to remain mistress in her own household. Mita is shocked but finally consents.

What we have is a Machiavellian exercise in

diplomacy that resolves the problem without a trace of scandal. The play has all the elements of a farce; yet we do not laugh at Uncle Simone (as we do at Machiavelli's Nicia); he is anything but ludicrous in our eyes. He is, in fact, himself a victim, like everyone else around him, of a closed society where rigorous tradition and conventions exact a heavy toll on poor and rich alike.

The paradox of the comic turned into pathos is wrought into a striking tapestry of contradictions, a rich layering of tragic and humorous in *Enrico IV*. In this play, *il sentimento del contrario* in given large dramatic expression. There is something comic about a masked pageant that extends to a lifetime of play-acting; in the adjustments servants have to make when they are hired to play 11th-century "retainers." We laugh when those already familiar with the rules, properly dressed in 11th century costumes, express consternation at the appearance of a a new member of the "staff" in 16th-century attire: he has mistakenly assumed his "role" to be that of a retainer in Shakespeare's time and is rushed off to change. There is humor also in the stratification of deception, beginning with the cosmetic effort of the Marchesa to look younger, and ending with the deception of portraits of figures in 11^{h} century costumes side by side with real life figures in those same costumes, posturing as still-life paintings. Even the "emperor's" madness has its comic side in our awareness that he regained his memory several years earlier and is now playing the role on another level.

But even as we laugh at scenes like these, we realize that the protagonist who has set up this elaborate fiction is not to be laughed at. His role-playing is a deliberate mask to shield him from the world that has betrayed him. He lashes out at his old rival and enemy, Belcredi, when the latter shows up with several other old "friends" to shock the "emperor" out of the past into the present. The play ends tragically when he fatally stabs Bencredi, his former rival for Matilda's affection, now her lover. That irrevocable action forces "Henry" back into the role he had momentarily cast aside. As a result of that confrontation, he deliberately resumes the fiction that had played itself out years earlier, when he had regained the memory lost when he fell from his horse in a *mardi gras* 11th-century pageant — a fall attributed to his old enemy and rival. In this extraordinary play, Pirandello presses *il sentimento del contrario* to its absolute limits, and beyond.

This new humor is integral to Pirandello's new vision of the stage, not something added when needed for laughter or comic relief but a substantive element of that vision, in which the protagonist leads the way to insight and greater self-awareness. Toward the end of *L'Umorismo*, Pirandello has this to say about the process:

> Let us consider the construction that illusion builds for each of us, that is, the construction that each of us makes of himself through the work of illusion. Do we see ourselves in our true and genuine reality, as we really are, or rather as what we should like to be? By means of a spontaneous internal device, a product of secret tendencies and unconscious imitation, do we not in good faith believe ourselves to be different from what we essentially are? And we think, act, and live according to this fictitious, and yet sincere, interpretation of ourselves.

Humor lies in the paradox that defines those two extremes: what you would like to be and what you really are. The movement between the two is characterized by a variety of overtones, colors, textures: comedy, satire, laughter, symbolic metaphorical effects — in short, the entire spectrum of human emotions and reactions. Pirandello explains that

> reflection, indeed, can reveal this illusory construction to the comic writer and to the satirist as well as to the humorist. But the comic writer will merely laugh, being content to deflate this metaphor of ourselves created by spontaneous illusion; the satirist will feel disdain

towards it; the humorist does neither: through the ridiculousness of the discovery, he will see the serious and painful side; he will disassemble the construction, but not solely to laugh at it; and, instead of feeling disdain, he will rather, in his laughter, feel compassion.[10]

Humor and pathos, and all that is connected with them, are the content of the *sentimento del contrario*. The paradox they represent is the heartbeat of the Pirandellian soul, which is forever struggling to maintain a delicate balance between the daily contradictions of life, the basic impulse to find a fixed base and "objective correlatives" and the even stronger impulse to flow with the inevitable pull of change.

> The oneness of the soul contradicts the historical concept of the human soul. Its life is a changing equilibrium; it is a continual awakening and obliterating of emotions, tendencies, and ideas; an incessant fluctuating between contradictory terms, and an oscillating between such extremes as hope and fear, truth and falsehood, beauty and ugliness, right and wrong, etc. If in the obscure view of the future a bright plan of action suddenly appears or the flower of pleasure is vaguely seen to shine, soon there also appears our memory of the past, often dim and sad, to avenge the rights of experience; or our sulky and unruly sense of the present will intervene to restrain our spiritual imagination. This conflict of memories, hopes, forebodings, perceptions, and ideals, can be seen as a struggle of various souls which are all fighting among themselves for the exclusive and final power over our personality. . . . Life is a continual flux which we try to stop, to fix in stable and determined forms, both inside and outside ourselves, because we are already fixed forms, forms which move in the midst of other immobile forms and which however can follow the flow of life until the movement, gradually slowing and becoming more and more rigid, eventually ceases. The forms in which we seek to stop, to fix in ourselves this constant flux are the concepts, the ideals with which we would like consistently to comply, all the fictions we create for ourselves, the conditions, the state in which we tend to

stabilize ourselves. But within ourselves, in what we call the soul and is the life in us, the flux continues, indistinct under the barriers and beyond the limits we impose as a means to fashion a consciousness and a personality for ourselves. In certain moments of turmoil all these fictitious forms are hit by the flux and collapse miserably under its thrust; and even what does not flow under the barrier and beyond the limits — that which is distinctly clear to us and which we have carefully channelled into our feelings, into the duties we have imposed upon ourselves, into the habits we have marked out for ourselves — in certain moments of floodtide, overflows and upsets everything.[11]

I think it relevant that *L'Umorismo* ends with references to Copernicus, who "disassembles . . . the haughty image we had formed [of the universe]," Leopardi, who wrote a magnificent satire on the subject, and the telescope "which dealt us the *coup de grace*: another infernal little mechanism which could pair up with the one nature chose to bestow on us." Humoristic reflection in this case suggests that we invented the telescope "so as not to be inferior." But are we, really?

Is man really as small as he looks when we see him through an inverted telescope? If he can understand and conceive of his infinite smallness, it means that he understands and conceives of the infinite greatness of the universe. How, then, can one say that man is small?[12]

With these remarks, Pirandello raises us, and his work, to a new level of awareness, where comedy and pathos become part of the universal paradox that is life itself.

NOTES

1. *On Humor.* Introduced, Translated, and Annotated by Antonio Illiano and Daniel P. Testa. Studies in Comparative Literature, Number 58 (The University of North Carolina Press, Chapel Hill, 1974).

2. In *Views of Humor*, edited by Harry Levin, Harvard English Studies, 3 (Harvard University Press, Cambridge).

3. *Ibid.*, pp 20-32.

4. In Silvio D'Amico, *Storia del teatro italiano* (Milano). English translation, "Pirandello's Introduction to the Italian Theater," by Anne Paolucci, in *The Genius of the Italian Theater*, ed. Eric Bentley (Mentor Books/New American Library, New York etc., 1964).

5. Olga Wester Russell, *Humor in Pascal* (The Christopher Publishing House. North Quince, MA, 1977), pp. 160-161.

6. *On Humor*, pp. 95-96.

7. *Ibid.*, p. 115.

8. *Ibid.*, pp. 144-145.

9. See, "Pirandello's *Liolà* and Machiavelli's *Mandragola*" later in this volume.

10. *On Humor*, p. 132.

11. *Ibid.*, pp. 136-137.

12. *Ibid.*, pp. 141-142.

COMEDY AND PARADOX IN PIRANDELLO'S PLAYS (AN HEGELIAN PERSPECTIVE)

The insistence of the intruders in *Six Characters in Search of an Author* to have the "professional" actors replace the play being rehearsed with their own personal melodrama may provoke laughter at first, but the story they tell is not laughable. They provide a script of sorts, dramatizing what they consider to be the key moment in their sad tale, but — according to them — the "professional" actors do not, nor will they ever be able to do that drama justice. By this time, our laughter is contained.

In a reverse but relevant contest, Shakespeare's Hamlet marvels that a mere player could express so well the passion that is festering inside himself, as though he, the actor, were the true victim, as portrayed in the script Hamlet has written for him. Pirandello's Father, like Hamlet, demands that the "professional" actors depict on stage the painful moment he has isolated in *his* script, and that they do so as convincingly as possible. He asks them to assume the temper and mood reflected in the script, in much the same way that Hamlet asks the visiting actors to follow *his* directions. Hamlet is pleased with the result he has engineered. The Father, in Pirandello's play, is not — raising implicitly a whole battery of questions about the possibility of communication on any level, the role of the actor, the limits of the stage, etc. At the end of the play, we, of course, applaud both the actors who played the "characters" as well as the "professional" actors, recognizing in this play (in spite of intriguing similarities with Shakespeare's) a daring *tour-de-force* altogether different from *Hamlet*.

Pirandello's own version of *Hamlet* is, of course,

First appeared in Modern Drama, *Vol. XX, No. 4, December 1997, pp. 321-340. (Revised.)*

Enrico IV (The Emperor Henry IV), in which the layering of roles, masks, costumes, time, history, etc., strains the paradox of *il sentimento del contrario* — Pirandello's definition of his new brand of humor — to its absolute limits.

What I have described is remarkably consonant with the argument put forward by the German philosopher Hegel: that the dissolution of art in the modern world coincides with that moment in history when individual freedom has been fully articulated. Hegel notes that it is dramatic comedy that comes into play at that time. Two brief subsections in his *Aesthetik* focus on this topic: "Die komische Behandlung der Zufälligkeit,"[1] ("The Comic Treatment of Contingency"[2]) and "Der subjektive Humor"[3] ("Subjective Humor"[4]). In them, he argues that art's dissolution comes finally not with a tragic bang or a melodramatic whimper but with laughter. At that moment

> it is the artist himself who enters the material, with the result that his chief activity, by the power of subjective notions, flashes of thought, striking modes of interpretation, consists in destroying and dissolving everything that proposes to make itself objective and win a firm shape for itself in reality, or that seems to have such a shape already in the external world.[5]

At the very end of his long lectures on aesthetics, after he has reviewed the entire progression of the arts from architecture through poetry, from the symbolic and classical through the romantic and modern, Hegel speaks finally of dramatic comedy in terms that make me think as much of Pirandello's comic creations as it does of Shakespeare's.

Hegel takes care to explain that there is a "clash of opposites" both in comedy and tragedy. In tragedy, the result is the destruction of the characters who sustain the opposition through one-sided willfulness or in a profound internal conversion that involves acceptance of what had been most seriously resisted previously. In comedy, instead, the characters dissolve the world around them into laughter, yet rise above it all, their subjective personality persisting well-assured.[6]

Distinguishing the laughable from the comical, Hegel adds:

> The comical as such implies an infinite light-heartedness and confidence felt by someone raised altogether above his own inner contradiction, not bitter or miserable in it at all: this is the bliss and ease of a man who, being sure of himself, can bear the frustrations of his aims and achievements. . . . A truly *tragic* action necessarily presupposes either a live conception of individual freedom and independence or at least an individual's determination and willingness to accept freely and on his own account the responsibility for his own act and its consequences, and for the emergence of *comedy* there must have asserted itself in a still higher degree the free right of the subjective personality and its self-assured dominion.[7]

A. C. Bradley, the great Shakespearean critic, saw — with Hegel's help — the essence of comedy embodied in Shakespeare's Falstaff,[8] whose wealth of spirit makes what is substantial emerge out of contingency with effortless, unostentatious lightness of expression which, paradoxically, in its very triviality expresses precisely what Hegel describes as "the supreme idea of depth."[9] He would have agreed also with Pirandello's notion of *il sentimento del contrario* and the intriguing correspondences it suggests in the indissoluble paradox between the comic Falstaff who drinks and cavorts with Prince Hal and the later Falstaff, rejected by Hal when he becomes Henry V.

In Hegel's discussion, as in Bradley's, and in the characters created by Pirandello, comedy emerges as the great democratic equalizer. Hegel explains that in civilized societies of which we have record, art that draws its materials and especially its characters from the lower classes tends almost invariably to be comic, for it cannot make the deeds of people externally restricted (as the lower classes are on all sides) seriously tragic. The lower-class character can "put on airs" of importance, but he cannot *be* important. If he persists in putting on such airs, he becomes comical. Comic characters have the right to spread themselves in whatever way they wish and can do so claiming an independence of action which — because of their restricted potential — is immediately annihilated by what they are, by their inner and outer dependence. "But, above all," says Hegel,

> this assumed self-reliance founders on external conditions and the distorted attitude of individuals to them. The power of those conditions is on a totally different level for the lower classes from what it is for rulers and princes.[10]

Hegel is not saying that the comic is limited to the lower classes; he is merely pointing out that lower-class characters have a potentially comic effectiveness. For example, a lower-class type with money, who imagines that money will take him out of the lower class culturally, someone like old Nicia in Machiavelli's *Mandragola*, is this kind of character. Molière's M. Jourdain is another. And so on.

For Hegel, comedy assumes a high dramatic importance, side by side with tragedy, as the vehicle for "pathos," which he defines as the "proper center, the true domain of art."[11] In discussing what he calls the "dissolution of the classical form of art," he anticipates *il sentimento del contrario* in the opposition between abiding spiritual values and external contingency — noting at the same time that the perception of such opposition, in itself, is merely prosaic: it takes us out of the world of art. It is comedy that resolves or *dissolves* that opposition artistically, reversing roles, showing the sham of good intentions and the positive value of social aberrations within that context.

> Of this kind of art [he writes] an example is comedy as Aristophanes among the Greeks has handled it without anger, in pure and serene . . . relation to the most essential spheres in the world of his time."[12]

Hegel goes on to extend his observations on

comedy and the lower classes to painting, using examples from the Germans and Dutch, where the subject is often taken from the crudest and most vulgar levels of society. Such paintings, he notes, offer us scenes

> so completely penetrated by . . . cheerfulness . . . that the real subject matter is not vulgarity, which is just vulgar and vicious, but this cheerfulness . . . roguish and comic . . . the Sunday of life which equalizes everything and removes all evil.[13]

The comic aspect, he explains, cancels what is bad and vulgar and leaves a very *positive* feeling.

Pirandello's comedy is that kind of paradox: it is inextricably combined with pathos, raising what might be construed as unconventional, vulgar, or simply prosaic into the realm of art. We first see this conversion clearly in Liolà, that amoral rogue who, in answer to Uncle Simone's charge that he is after the old man's money, can sing a song which is "the Sunday of life, which equalizes everything and removes all evil." Eric Bentley notes correctly that we must enter Pirandello's world through *Liolà*, where we already can distinguish the genuine Pirandello from modern Pirandellianism, which is *pseudo*-Pirandellian because it does not have beneath it, around and above it, that Sicilian "Sunday" comedy that gives this early play its cheerful positive aspect. Pirandello's comedy, as early as in *Liolà*, accords with Hegel's description in its *redemption* of the vulgar and the bad.

It also recognizes the need to differentiate between what Hegel describes as *dramatis personae* who are "comical in themselves or only in the eyes of the audience."[14] Only the former, Hegel tells us (agreeing with Aristotle), can be considered comical in the strict sense, as opposed to the merely laughable. Plautus and Terence preferred the latter; and although on a certain level their "comedy" has continued to be popular down through the centuries, it is Shakespeare (Hegel tells us) who shows us the full potential of comedy as high art with characters who, in the mature comedies, are aggrandized and enhanced.

> Stephano, Trinculo, Pistol, and the absolute hero of them all, Falstaff, remain sunk in their vulgarity, but at the same time they are shown as men of intelligence, . . . enabling them to have an entirely free existence, and, in short, to be what great men they are. . . . In Shakespeare we find justification, no condemnation, but only an observation of . . . universal fate, . . . and from that independent standpoint they see everything perish, themselves included, as if they saw it all happening outside themselves.[15]

Pirandello certainly must have appreciated Shakespeare's *ipsissima verba*, where he has Falstaff say:

> The brain of this foolish-compounded clay, man, is not able to invent anything that intends to laughter, more than I invent or is invented on me. I am not only witty in myself, but the cause that wit is in other men.[16]

Pirandello does not linger on the comic genius of Shakespeare in *L'Umorismo*, although he does cite with approval Giorgio Arcoleo's view that Hamlet is an instance of the first phase of humor, which consists in being able to "*laugh at one's own thought.*"[17]

In his long essay on the history of the Italian theater, Pirandello dwells on that moment in history when that theater found new vitality in the *commedia dell'arte*. "We see there," he writes, "actors . . . who begin by writing the comedies they later perform, comedies at once more theatrical because not written in the isolated study," but in the theater itself.

> The transitory, impassioned life of the Theater must have taken such full possession of them that the only interest left to them was that of the spectacle itself — a complete absorption in the quality of the performance and communication with the audience. They are no longer authors, but they are no longer actors, in the true sense of the word.

He recognized in the *commedia dell'arte* not only the

equalizer Hegel had described in writing about the dissolution effected by comedy in the modern world: what it did to shatter the rigidity of the Renaissance inheritance was analogous to what his new theater had done in challenging a dramatic art that had lost contact with its living origins. For an antecedent, he points to Goldoni, who learned the lesson of the *commedia dell'arte* even as Molière and Shakespeare already had. But Goldoni had hit on something else of even greater significance:

> ... we will never discover the true Goldoni if we fix our attention on the characters that, according to the fashion of the time, he too tried to create — the good-natured boor, the gambler, the miser, etc. They are indeed marvelous, but in the comedies in which they appear as protagonists the truly great author reveals himself, on the contrary, in the subordinate characters, one of whom — the little housemaid, for example — suddenly becomes, like Mirandolina, the center of a comedy of her own, and many others come forward, en masse, to stand there and bicker freely in the streets of Chioggia.[18]

Read as a revelation of Pirandello's view of drama, the essay on the Italian theater, as well as the one on humor, is surely invaluable in interpreting his plays. But we must not mistake either one for an empirically-based theory, although what he describes in those two essays is obviously in accord with his new theater.

In my own view, Pirandello's brand of humor could not have had full scope until he turned from narrative to drama. The whole world's a stage! the dramatic imagination cries. It is in drama that *il sentimento del contrario* is best felt, best mirrors our own paradoxical selves on the stage of life, on which we all strut and fret our given time.

The paradoxical humor that emerges on the Pirandellian stage cracks the solidity of the subject, till decomposition is inevitable. Situations, characters, events, thoughts — all are overwhelmed, pinned down with conditionals, hammered till they are shattered, at least in our reflection, into myriad mirrored fragments. If we attempt to piece the fragments together like a jigsaw puzzle, what we get is not a cracked impression of the original, but the personality of the comic artist who has made it all his very own, precisely in order to dissolve its apparent rigidity.

In that perception, we are reminded of the Delphic Oracle's command to "know thyself." The cleared stage allows us to see ourselves in rational reflection. We *are* what reflective reasoning shows us to be. Yet, when that viewing has been done in any society, a time inevitably follows when the reflection hardens so as to become impenetrable; and then, instead of being perceived as a rational reflection, rationally real in itself, it becomes merely a reflecting surface in which we imagine we see our subjective selves reflected as opposite. The comic spirit, as Hegel noted, shatters that hardness, dissolves it: comedy is always a reaction to some other form of drama, whether ceremonial in the religious sense, or tragic.

Pirandello, coming late to the task, does this sort of comic work with a thoroughness that is positively exhaustive. But what exactly is it that he views in this exhaustive way? It is absurd to say — bearing in mind that we are talking about a man who invaded the early twentieth-century European stage like a conqueror with his *Six Characters in Search of an Author* — that it is life in general. By the time he begins to stage his plays, he has already swept away mere life as an object of artistic and critical reflection. It is out of the depths of mirrored opposites that he draws his *dramatis personae*, the embodiments of his *sentimento del contrario*.

The Sicilian realism of his early *Liolà*, its easy and traditional structure, the recognizable types — at once characteristic and unique — may mislead us, in the light of his later work. into regarding it as a struggling toward form, a preliminary effort of a gifted playwright not yet sure of himself. Nothing could be farther from the truth. *Liolà* — like Shakespeare's early but masterful *Julius Caesar* — is already a perfect expression of what will be the dramatist's special idiom, his unusual, even eccentric style. Pirandello, of course, had Machiavelli's *Mandragola* vividly before him (there can be no doubt about it): *Liolà* is a romanticized aberration of that perverse and bitter redoing of Livy's story of the virtuous Lucrece. Already there is a paradox working itself to the surface in Pirandello's choice of subject. It is the same basic story as that of Livy and Machiavelli; but the perception and the feelings of the opposite are inspired by Machiavelli's bitter realism, adapted to a new purpose which redeems the negative, almost unbearable Machiavellian insights into human nature at its worst. Pirandello turns things right side up and upside down again in this early work, introducing — in the guise of Realism — the kind of complex and paradoxical characters that will people his later plays.

In Liolà, the main protagonist of this early play, Pirandello has created a god-image, a modern Pan who bestows his gifts with charitable abandonment. He makes girls pregnant, but there is no malice in him. He respects the societal order, the lines of demarcation between respectability and personal indulgence. The women he makes pregnant are willing to accept the consequences of their behavior. There are no confrontations, no reversals of essential values in these casual encounters. Liolà, in spite of his poverty, even offers to marry those who become pregnant by him. When they refuse, he and his mother take in and raise the children he has fathered.

His happy though somewhat unconventional life is shattered when his poor but honest childhood sweetheart Mita — forced to marry old Uncle Simone, whose wealth will insure her future and that of the heir she is expected to produce — is threatened by a plot by Tuzza, a shrewd village girl who happens to be carrying Liolà's bastard. Tuzza and her mother come forward, when Mita (like Uncle Simone's first wife) does not conceive, to offer the old man Tuzza's bastard by Liolà — in exchange for certain considerations. He agrees to the arrangement.

When he hears about Tuzza's plan, Liolà is furious. Bent on revenge or, more properly, moved by by righteousness, he works out his own counterplot. He tells Mita she must let him give her the heir Uncle Simone craves but will never be able to give her. He's much too old and obviously impotent: his first wife never conceived in all the years they were married. Mita must counter Tuzza's wicked plot by producing a child of her own in the same way Tuzza produced the one she has offered Uncle Simone. Mita is shocked, but Liolà's arguments, although blunt and cruel, are unanswerable. She can't expect another virgin birth, he tells her. If she doesn't produce the wanted heir, Tuzza will take over: Mita will be reduced to a stranger in her own house, having to put up with Tuzza's presence in the house and destined to raise Tuzza's bastard as her own. Mita finally agrees.

In Pascalian terms, Liolà is planning to rescue Mita from an intolerable future and to make Tuzza *le depeur dupé*, the Bible's deceived deceiver. Mita is a victim, of course, but in taking on the role in which Liolà has cast her, she too takes on a paradoxical posture. She must be selfish in order to be unselfish. She must submit to Liolà not out of personal desire (although she loves him as deeply as he loves her) but because the essential values below the surface of respectability must be preserved. The threat she faces calls for quick thinking and action. She herself is too naïve, committed to the absolute code of morality in which she has been raised. She is not ready to act as Liolà wants her to, as Tuzza has. But when her very existence in the established social framework is threatened — and not only hers, but Uncle Simone's too, in the end — she allows herself to be drawn into a conspiracy not unlike that of Tuzza's. But of course, in Mita's case, and Liolà's, their counterplot is not on the same level's as Tuzza's: the opposite is also true — just as it is also true that in producing a child by Liolà,

Mita is no more self-indulging or selfish than he is.

In Liolà, Pirandello has created a god-image, a modern Pan who bestows his gifts with charitable ease, who draws women to him without trying. He makes girls pregnant, but there is no malice in him: he is not in the true sense a seducer. He respects the societal order and offers to marry them in every case. When they refuse him, he and his mother take in and raise the children he has fathered. There is no substantive reversal of essential values in these casual encounters and the adjustments that result.

Uncle Simone is the modern equivalent of Machiavelli's Nicia — but how utterly different is his comic posture, if indeed we can call it that! And how paradoxical is his final decision to accept, in effect, what Nicia in *Mandragola* consents to, thinking that he has outwitted the clever *imbroglioni* who in fact have outwitted *him*. In one way they are very much alike: they both refuse to admit that they are impotent.

In this scenario, Uncle Simone is comic, if at all, in his generic role of the childless impotent rich old man, bent on an heir, much as Nicia is; but he is not a fool. Unlike Nicia, who is comic "in the eyes of the audience," Uncle Simone suggests an unexpressed awareness of a complex situation, an implicit confrontation with self. Although in agreeing to accept Tuzza's child as his own he announced, in a way, his willingness to be cuckolded, there are no *imbroglioni*, no self-serving mercenary and lecherous strangers to hoodwink him and laugh behind his back, as in Machiavelli's play. In his own mind, Uncle Simone might well have argued: "If only God's grace would fill Mita as it had filled Mary! But I need a child of my own, not another Christ. If only my healthy young wife Mita could be filled . . . as Tuzza was filled . . . so that I could have a child by her, so that I could claim that child as my heir . . . as I am ready to claim Tuzza's bastard!" All this is left unspoken of course; and perhaps Uncle Simone never even entertained such thoughts: but surely they are suggested in the funny but sad game we are watching.

Mita will, in fact, offer him an heir he can claim as his own, no questions asked. If he is tempted to draw a parallel with Tuzza's situation, he gives no sign or, more precisely, Pirandello doesn't give him the chance to express it. With Liolà's enigmatic solution, Tuzza's nefarious scheme backfires. A terrible wrong has been made right.

Somehow, Pirandello makes all this believable and acceptable by means of a complex structure of opposites: *e.g.* seduction / non-seduction, intrigue / counter-intrigue, cupidity / love, selfishness and greed / self-protective sentimentality, human initiative / divine coincidence, and so on. Paradox is the very texture of the play.

There is something clearly exhaustive about such humor in *Six Characters*, as well. The actors cast as the six "real-life" people are not supposed to be actors. They represent what the "professional" actors are supposed to play on stage, once they have a script. As we watch, we come to realize that communication is virtually impossible between the two groups. We realize that the "professional" actors can never live up to the expectations of the "characters." Pirandello has expanded here on the same paired perception of opposites noted in *Liolà*.

At first, the insistence of the "characters" on the smallest details is funny; their exaggerations easily provoke laughter; but the story they weave is not laughable. They provide a script of sorts of part of that story, of what they consider the key moment in it, but — according to them — the "professional" actors do not, will never be able to do it justice. We're reminded, in a reverse but relevant context, of Hamlet's speech on the subject of acting, his marveling that a mere player could call up so much passion, assume the aspect of grief so realistically, while he, Hamlet, who has real cause for grief, cannot bring himself to express it. Pirandello's Father, like Hamlet, demands that the "professional" actors depict on stage the painful moment he has isolated in the script he has provided, and that they do so as convincingly as possible. He asks them to assume the temper and mood described in his script, in much the same way that Hamlet asked the visiting actors to follow *his* script. Hamlet is pleased with the result he engineered. The Father in Pirandello's play is not — raising implicitly a whole battery of questions about the possibility of communication on any level, the role of the actor, the limits of the stage, etc. etc. Those questions remain, although at the end of the play, we applaud both the actors who played the "characters" and the "professional" actors.

Pirandello's own version of *Hamlet*, as we shall see, is *Enrico IV*, which many critics consider his masterpiece. The layering of roles, masks, costumes, time, history in that extraordinary play presses *il sentimento del contrario* to its absolute limits, and beyond.

In *Così è (se vi pare) (Right You Are! [If You Think So])* Pirandello undermines appearances and conventions in a different way, demolishing facts as they are put forward with the persistence of a grand inquisitor, until we are forced to recognize that nothing can be taken for granted. A cumulative effect is produced by arguments that spiral to some kind of "proof" only to be cleverly and unambiguously knocked down. What appears as rational scaffolding simply doesn't hold up.

Laudisi, the Socratic skeptic (without the redeeming Socratic assurance of internal conviction) has often been described as the spokesman for Pirandello, the character who best approximates the playwright's views, especially with regard to "reality" vs. "illusion." He is, actually, the *pseudo*-Pirandellian, the empiricist *par excellence* who weighs and measures facts as they surface, uncovering their inconsistencies and contradictions. He takes delight in provoking exposure, not really prepared to track down the truth but insisting on questioning and destroying appearances, knocking down suppositions that pass as hard facts. He is the balance that keeps the scale from tipping to one side or the other. At a certain moment, however, skepticism must give way to something else. Pirandello builds the dramatic confrontations around the two people who are truly committed, who have *willed* the truth — each in his own way.

Two committed characters, two contradictory assertions. Where does the truth lie?

There can be no answer at all, so long as the question is phrased in that way, so long as the answer is sought in another external *fact* or in another combination of *circumstances*. Certainly Laudisi offers no answer. He simply dramatizes what is negative. Signore Ponza and his mother-in-law Signora Frola cannot provide the kind of answer others expect. Their positions are diametrically opposed, and yet they strike sympathetic chords which remind us that they are not very far apart in the quality of their commitment. But surely the answer may be found in Signora Ponza, the object of all the concern and all the detective work. Surely, she can tell us who she is?

Pirandello drives us from one set of facts to another and another, until there are no facts left to consult; and then, finally, he presents us with the *embodied* fact, the one person who can give us a direct answer. And here, of course, Pirandello's *sentimento del contrario* becomes dramatically immediate and visual. Signora Ponza turns out to be the ultimate, absolute paradox, the last in a series of incredible statements which are ambiguous in the same way that the oracular utterances of the Delphic priestess were both ambiguous and potentially true. Signora Ponza acknowledges the paradox of her own essential being by reiterating her relationship to Ponza and to Signora Frola. What is she in herself? The *certainty* of their conviction: she is Ponza's wife and Signora Frola's daughter. Reality in the common sense has been penetrated, exhausted, and dismissed in those two assurances. As for the others who want to reach *out* instead of reaching *inside* themselves for meaning: I can only be for them (she says) an abortive fact. The veiled woman need not unveil for the man who willfully insists she is his second wife or for the woman who just as convincingly insists she is her daughter, but to those who still look to *external facts* for direction and assurance, she can only be a clever trick, an incomplete notion, a mystery.

The humor in this play (as in *Liolà*), carries with it a great deal of irony — and not just the verbal kind we find in Laudisi or in Diego Cenci in *Ciascuno a suo modo (Each in His Own Way)*, but also irony of situation, particularly in the contradictory postures which the Aguzzi and their friends assume as each set of seemingly irrefutable facts comes to light. Here, as in *Liolà*, the turning of the tables has an obvious comic effect; but in the larger context, that effect is mitigated by pathos and compassion.

One of the best examples of the interweaving of irony, laughter, and pathos is Pirandello's one-act play, *All'uscita (At the Exit)*, where half-baked ghosts must wait for their one overwhelming earthly wish to be fulfilled before they can be swallowed up into merciful oblivion. The Fat Man (another version of Uncle Simone) is the first to go. His great wish had been to see his wife cry at least once, instead of always laughing hysterically. When she comes rushing in, just killed by her lover, crying as she follows a cart on which a little boy sits, the child she always wanted and never had, the Fat Man's wish has been fulfilled and he disappears, his walking stick falling to the ground. The Philosopher alone remains on stage, condemned, one suspects, like the woman, to an eternity similar to that of Tantalus, reaching out but never grasping what he most craves, ultimate Truth.

There is a comic frenzy about this one-act play, a great deal in it that is laughable and rather wild. And yet, the total effect is powerfully pathetic, in the Pirandellian sense of the word. Its novelty can best be assessed, I think, if we compare it with Thornton Wilder's *Our Town*, which many have said was inspired by *All'uscita*. Both plays deal with the connection between the living and the dead, but Pirandello's focus, unlike Wilder's, is on the subtle juxtaposition of comedy and pathos rather than sentimental memories.

It is in *Enrico IV* that paradox and comedy are given large dramatic expression. There is subtle humor in the masked pageant extended to a lifetime of play-acting; humor in Henry's servants having to change into 11th-century costumes when they come on the job every day, in the real-life figures standing in front of portraits for which they seem to have posed. There is humor too, under the pretense of "madness," in Henry's rewriting of history according to his own reading of events: his account of the real Emperor's journey to Canossa to ask the Pope's forgiveness.

There is also the nervous humor of a modern script that is being revised even as we watch; in the incongruity between the outside world and Henry's isolated, restricted personal one, which has suddenly been invaded by his erstwhile friends, who soon discover they have stumbled into something too big to handle. There is humor in Henry's effort to maintain the fiction of the Emperor, to continue to play the part, even when that fiction no longer is needed.

Like Hamlet — who is never farther from the revenge he has promised to carry out than he is during the play scene, when he realizes that he cannot tell anyone why he should kill the king without sounding mad and breaking his promise to the Ghost, and that if he *does* kill Claudius he will appear to be the very same kind of usurper he has judged his uncle to be — Pirandello's Henry already has deeply embedded in him, the inexorable ending of his own play. That ending is consistent with all the rest. What had been judged earlier to be some sort of madness now becomes an assumed madness, never again to be set aside. Of course, madness in the true sense is never a question in *Enrico IV* (just as it is never a question in *Hamlet*); it is simply one of the many masks behind which the pathos of self-reflection is hidden from the world.

Pirandello's mood in *Enrico IV* is much like that of Shakespeare's Prospero, even more than that of Cotrone in his last play, *I Giganti della montagna* (*The Montain Guants*). What Goldoni gives us in the streets of Chioggia and what Henry gives us in his multilevel scenario is as marvelous, surely, as the magic storm worked up by Prospero to frighten his prisoners and teach them a lesson. Ariel reports back to his master that the charms have indeed worked wonders; the shipwrecked victims of Prospero's temper are huddled together, so full of sorrow and fear that

> if you now beheld them, your affections
> would become tender.

Prospero, who for the moment has only the *perception* of the opposite, replies simply:

> Dost thou think so, spirit?

Ariel disarms him, undermining the detached cold security of the puppet-master, by answering:

> Mine would, sir, were I human.

And Prospero replies:

> And mine shall.
> Hast thou, which art but air, a touch, a feeling
> Of their afflictions, and shall not myself,
> One of their kind, that relish all as sharply
> Passion as they, be kindlier mov'd than thou art?[19]

The art of Pirandello's *il sentimento del contrario* is to bring us where Ariel's reply brings Prospero.

Comedy and paradox are the heartbeat of Pirandello's dramatic universe. Its pulse is captured by such characters as the detached skeptic Laudisi, the involved skeptic Diego Cenci, the vulnerable skeptic Henry IV as well as many other creations of Pirandello's *fantasia*. They remind us that we are not one but many contradictory things.

In final analysis, it is not Laudisi but Henry IV who comes closest to Pirandello himself, who wore at least as many masks each several hour as Shakespeare himself wore and reminds us of, in the words of his most celebrated creation, Hamlet:

> What a piece of work is a man! how noble in reason! how infinite in faculties! in form and moving how express and admirable! in action how like an angel! in apprehension how like a god! the beauty of the world, the paragon of animals! And yet to me what is this quintessence of dust?[20]

Or, in George Herbert's Pirandellian lines:

> O what a thing is man! how far from power,
> From settled peace and rest!
> He is some twenty several men at least
> Each several hour.[21]

NOTES

1. See G. W. F. Hegel, *Aesthetik*, eds. H. G. Hotho and Friedrich Bassenge (Frankfurt am Main, 1965), Vol. I, pp. 565-567.

2 See G. W. F. Hegel, *Aesthetics*, translated by T. M. Knox (Oxford University Press, Oxford, 1975), Vol. I, pp. 590-592.

3. *Aesthetik*, Vol. I, pp. 574-576.

4. *Aesthetics*, Vol. I, pp. 600-602.

5. *Ibid.*, pp. 600-601.

6. *Ibid.*, Vol. II, p. 1205.1199.

7. *Ibid.*

8. See Bradley's "The Rejection of Falstaff" in *Oxford Lectures on Poetry* ((Macmillan & Co, Ltd., London, 1950), pp. 245-275.

9. *Aesthetics*, Vol. I, p. 602.

10. *Ibid.*, p. 192

11. *Ibid.*, p. 232.

12. *Ibid.*, p. 511.

13. *Ibid.*, Vol. II, pp. 886-887.

14. *Ibid.*, p. 1220.

15. *Ibid.*, Vol. I, pp. 585-586.

16. William Shakespeare, *2 Henry IV*, I, ii, 8-12, in *The Complete Works of Shakespeare*, ed. George Lyman Kittredge (New York, 1936).

17. *On Humor*, introduced, translated and annotated by Antonio Illiano and Daniel P. Testa, Studies in Comparative Literature, Number 58 (University of North Carolina Press, Chapel Hill, 1974), p. 102.

18. "Pirandello's Introduction to the Italian Theater," translated by Anne Paolucci, in *Genius of the Italian Theater*, ed. Eric Bentley (Mentor Books/New American Library, New York, 1964), pp. 11-29. (See entire essay in Part Four.)

19. Shakespeare, *The Tempest*, V, I, 18-24

20. Shakespeare, *Hamlet*, II, ii, 316-322

21. George Herbert, "Giddiness," cited by James Thomson, "Sympathy," *Essays and Phantasies* (London, 1881) p. 242.

Dramatic Argument on Stage

Early criticism of Pirandello, which focused on what was described as his "cerebral" tendency — too much extraneous talk on stage — was no doubt prodded by what appeared to be an unresolved skepticism, the dichotomy of "reality vs. illusion." I need hardly point out that open-ended skepticism leads nowhere, both in real life and on the stage. Simplistic questioning would certainly not have revolutionized the European theater, as Pirandello's plays obviously did. To insist that he is merely indulging in an abstract questioning of the reality of things is to write off as incomprehensible the tremendous impact he had on the playwrights who followed him. Pirandello's theater is meant to *dispel* doubt and relativism. Contradictions are dramatized as argument, an integral and vital element of the action, part of the "process" that leads to truth and certainty and inextricably linked to the end product: the assertion of the *will*.

Good theater in every age makes effective use of argument. Antigone argues her point in Sophocles' play; so does Creon. Hamlet argues his doubts over and over again. Macbeth broods about deeds and their consequences. Beckett has Lucky parody the strained formal arguments of philosophy in *Waiting for Godot*. All good drama uses argument as an integral part of the stage action, and Pirandello is no exception. But what he does that is new and different is to present argument by means of a variety of masks and mirrors, as a series of oscillating extremes, forcing characters to recognize their own paradoxical premises.

Argument is the instrument of self-discovery in Pirandello's plays. It demolishes the familiar and the obvious. In the language of modern existentialist phenomenology, it forces us from simple consciousness to self-consciousness to identity, from mirrors to confrontations with mirrored images, to confrontations with others. This is not the language of relativism;

there is nothing cerebral about it. Through argument, Pirandello intends to *dispel* doubt and relativism; it is an integral and vital element of his plays, part of the Pirandellian "process" which — as Robert Brustein has noted — is as important as the end "product."

Our first task, then, is to reject the prevailing cliché. For Pirandello, *reality* is the internal self which comes to know itself in all its strengths and weaknesses through a Socratic dialectic; and *illusion* is the vast world of ready-to-wear habits to which most of us subscribe, the world outside us, the unexamined life.

In his early masterpiece, *Liolà*, Pirandello forces a Machiavellian argument to its inexorable conclusion — even though the very foundations of traditional society and values are threatened in the acceptance of that conclusion. In *La patente (The License)*, argument forces the easy logic of acceptance to its rigorous conclusion, turning prejudice against itself. In *All'uscita (At the Exit)*. abstract philosophizing is undermined with a dramatic examination of the limits of human love. In *La giarra (The Jar)*, argument is focused on a paradoxical situation that is essentially comic. In *Così è (se vi pare) (Right You Are! [If You Think So])* argument destroys conventional attitudes and shows how emotional and intellectual atrophy set in with passive acceptance of an unexamined world. In *Questa sera si recita a soggetto (Tonight We Improvise)*, argument serves — as in *Six Characters* — to measure the distance between assumed roles and living masks. In *La nuova colonia (The New Colony)*, argument tests abstract social ideals against the realities of an imperfect world. In *Lazzaro (Lazarus)*, argument puts faith to the same kind of test, submitting rote acceptance of God to the most difficult personal trials in order to gain true and lasting insight into love and goodness. In *Enrico IV (Henry IV)*, argument shatters the isolation of a self-designed personal world. In his last play, *I giganti della montagna (The Mountain Giants)*, argument defines the limits of art, particularly of dramatic art. In these and other plays, Pirandello dramatizes argument as a vital factor in the equation that traces the journey of life into the interior of self, in which the internal landscape — the thoughts, emotions, motivations, and ideas of individuals caught in a variety of situations — is translated into stage-worthy action. His premise is good theater, and his method is not open-ended discussion, not an easy relativism that underscores an obvious question, but an *assertion of the will* through a series of dialectical inversions and reversals. In this kind of dramatic methodology, writes Robert Corrigan, "appearances not only do not express reality, they contradict it, and the meaning of his plays is not to be found in appearance or reality but in the contradiction itself."

Some will say: Pirandello hit on something that worked for him and made good use of it. Well, that's true. But it's also true that the "something" he hit on was somewhat complex, hardly accidental — just as the clusters of images suggesting stunted growth, the killing of babes, mother's milk and blood, violent uprootings, vulnerable creatures, darkness, in Macbeth's self-made hell, could not possibly have been metaphors that Shakespeare hit on accidentally; just as Dante's child images at the top of Purgatory, the moment of rebirth, could not possibly be construed as accidental; just as Arthur Miller's premonitions of disaster, his Greek-type omens in *All My Sons* were not accidental; just as Albee's inversion of the Holy Trinity and the replica of the mansion as a symbol of infinity in *Tiny Alice* were not accidental. No author of any merit stumbles into his special language; it is honed deliberately to best reflect the content, in all its multifaceted variety. This is eminently true of Pirandello.

To understand the novelty of Pirandello's language and his use of dramatic argument, we must recognize in the term *reality* the internal self, in all its strengths and weaknesses, and in the word *illusion* the outside unexamined world, waiting to be made ours. We will be totally misled from Pirandello's purpose if, for example, we view the "theater plays" as simply clever role-playing. In emphasizing the impossibility of even the best actors to portray the family's sad story, The Father in *Six Characters* is underscoring the basic notion that self-awareness cannot be communicated: it must evolve internally. Is this relativism? Not at all. The mirrors of personal confrontations are dramatic assertions that nothing can be said that has not already been understood. The efforts of the six characters to act out their tragic story find, it is true, a ready convention in the stage; but what they are telling us, on and off that stage, in and out of that convention, is that the direction of communication is all wrong so long as a dichotomy exists. So long as the appeal is to actors who *impersonate* them, who remain outside the experience, communication will fail. In that context, argument can only be a dead-end.

The *process* of bringing the outside world into the internal landscape of the self is even clearer in *Ciascuno a suo modo (Each in His Own Way)*, the second of the three so-called "theater plays." There the stage drama and the "real-life" drama are superimposed, as it were, both part of the script. A third level of action is the "Choral Interludes," or intermissions, these too part of the script. During the latter, critics argue about the merits of the Pirandello play they are watching, while in another part of the stage lobby the protagonists of the "real-life" story Pirandello has dramatized and is actually being performed create their own dramatic diversion. In *Questa sera si recita a soggetto (Tonight We Improvise)*, the third of the "theater plays," we're treated to a play in the making, as it were: delays in raising the curtain, apologies and stories by the director (who comes out more than once to ask the audience to be patient), heated exchanges off and on stage before the play begins — or rather, before the *improvisation* begins (scripted of course).

In the kind of theater just described, dramatic dialectic inevitably replaces "statement" and argument defies logic and conventions.

Argument is already a key element in the one-act plays. In *La patente* (*The License*), the protagonist Chiarchiaro has been cursed by the villagers with the title of "iettatore," carrier of the evil eye, because of the misfortunes he and his family have suffered. Everyone avoids him, as though his condition is contagious. The poor man's pretty daughters can find no work, no one will have them; marriage for them is out of the question. Chiarchiaro's son, with three children of his own, must now provide for his father, his invalid mother, and his two sisters.

In his desperate efforts to find work of any kind, Chiarchiaro is insulted and driven away. The townspeople see him as the embodiment of back luck and do not want to be "infected" by him. In desperation, he resorts to an incredible and seemingly idiotic solution: he files suit against one of his chief tormentors. The Examining Magistrate calls him in to tell him he has no chance of winning his case: why bother? A trial will make him the laughing stock of the town. But Chiarchiaro stands his ground: he will not withdraw his suit. In fact (he tells them), he looks forward to the trial. The Magistrate and others who hear this are confused. Think of your family, they say; why put them through further pain by making a public spectacle of yourself?

In a masterful argument, Chiarchiaro explains that he intends to *lose* the case!

> Are you aware that I— I, Rosario Chiarchiaro — that I myself went to see Lorecchio to make sure that he has all the evidence he needs to win? In other words, I not only told him that I've known for more than a year about everyone making signs against the Evil Eye, and other more or less insulting gestures, whenever I go by, but I also gave him proofs, Your Honor, documented proofs — irrefutable evidence, you know, ir-re-fu-ta-ble — concerning the terrible events on which my reputation as a bearer of the Evil Eye is unshakably founded. Un-sha-ka-bly, Your Honor!

The Examining Magistrate is astounded. But Chiarchiaro is way ahead of him with a relentless and unanswerable logic of his own.

> I brought this case into court because I want official recognition of my power. Now to you understand? I want this terrible power of mine to be officially recognized, to be legally established.

He will turn the prejudices that have destroyed him to his advantage. The facts cited against him will be used to serve another end.

Conventional arguments are forced to their limits in Chiarchiaro's insistence that the trial be held. His ingenious plan turns the personal tragedy into high comedy, but the laughter it evokes is guarded. In insisting on a trial, he gains new confidence and power. He is no longer the victim. Official recognition will enable him to set up his own business, legally recognized as a *iettatore*. If people are so perverted in their Christian fellowship, so prejudiced that they can allow an entire family to starve, then they must be made to pay for their willful selfishness. Losing the case means the stamp of approval for what others have wrongly labeled him to be. He will put his legal "title" on calling cards, presenting them at the shops along the main thoroughfare. The owners, not wanting to lose business, will pay him to move off. In this way, Chiar-chiaro has insured a livelihood for himself. As in *Liolà*, the solution is neither expected nor ideal; but it is what others have brought about by their shortsightedness and meanness, what they have forced him to carve out for himself. When the others object to his bizarre plan, he argues:

> You think it's so unimportant? My whole life is at stake! I'm a ruined man, Your Honor! The poor father of an innocent family. For years I worked hard and honestly. They threw me out, kicked me into the gutter because they said I had the Evil Eye! In the gutter, with my wife a paralytic, bedridden for the past three years, and with two young daughters who, if you could see them, Your Honor, it would break your heart, they're so pretty, both of them. But no one will have anything to do with them because they're mine, you understand? and do your know what we live on now, all four of us? On the bread

my son takes out of his mouth, and he a family man with three children of his own to feed! How much longer do you think the poor boy can go on sacrificing himself for me? Your Honor, there's nothing left for me to do but go into business with this Evil Eye of mine. I'm forced to practice the only profession I have.

His argument is as clearsighted as his name implies. The money he will get, he tells his listeners, is simply a new kind of tax. The play ends with Chiarchiaro triumphantly asserting that he alone is responsible for the death of the Magistrate's pet goldfinch, which has toppled to the floor in its cage when a strong wind threw open the shutters of the room. Others rush in at the sound of the crash and draw back in horror at the sight of Chiarchiaro in his costume of rags, standing by the broken cage and the dead bird — "proof" of the power the others have attributed to him. They quickly hand him the money he demands, in order to avoid their being "infected" by similar bad luck. "You see?" Chiarchiaro cries out, "and I don't even have my license yet! Get on with the trial! I'm rich! I'm rich!" The terrible burden imposed on him has been transformed into a personal victory.

In *La giarra* (*The Jar*), dramatic argument rises out of the comic consequences of Uncle Dima's effort to repair a crack that has developed in a huge container used for storing olive oil. The jar belongs to Don Loló, a suspicious and argumentative landowner, who thinks he has been cheated and is getting ready to sue the people from whom he bought the jar. Dima, the expert repairman of such containers, is called in to fix it with a new adhesive he has perfected; but Don Loló insists on rivets as well. A new crises arises when Dima, having finished the repairs, realizes he can't get out of the jar because of the rivets Don Loló had insisted on adding. Don Loló is furious and blames Dima, who did not take into account the hump on his back, when he entered the jar. Predictably, he refuses to break the jar to set Dima free. He refers to the legal manual he carries with him at all times and calls in his lawyer, Scima, who tells him the obvious: he can't keep the tinker inside the jar indefinitely. As in *The License*, the confrontation evokes comic effects, the result, in this case, of Don Loló's literal reading of the law and Dima's refusal to pay for the jar that must be broken to get him out. Comedy reaches a peak when Dima sends his cronies for wine and cheese and roasted peppers. Frustrated beyond endurance, Don Loló kicks the jar and sends it rolling down a slope, where it ends up hitting a tree and cracking open. Dima comes out, yelling "I win! I win!"

Even in these two short plays, argument comes into focus as a creative madness which is full of pathos and yet comic as well.

In *Right You Are!* argument is honed to perfection within a larger framework in which facts and proofs are put through a series of tests. The play is a *reductio ad absurdum* of the reliability of facta and undermines the trust people place in them. There is no legal machinery here, such as we saw in the one-act plays just discussed, but the dramatic premise rests on the same rigorous reading of formal rules. Laudisi, the eternal skeptic, provides the major arguments in this case. As each piece of "evidence" surfaces and raises hopes that the truth will come to light, Laudisi shatters that illusion with his destructive logic. The only ones who seem confident in their contradictory assertions are Signore Ponza and his mother-in-law Signora Frola, whose daughter was Ponza's first wife. When all evidence has been eroded away and Signora Ponza is called on to identify herself — the one solid and unanswerable proof of identity — she admits paradoxically to being the second wife of Signor Ponza and Signora Frola's daughter. In herself, she mirrors what the others have made her out to be: an abortive fact. The reality of her existence lies in the *conviction* of those two people, even though to others their assertions seem contradictory. Pirandello has deftly reduced argument to a paradox, reiterating the basic notion that what is outside us remains extraneous.

In his Introduction to *Seven One-Act Plays of Pirandello*, William Murray, the translator, cites the playwright's words, that theater is a serious affair which

> demands the complete participation of the moral-human entity. It is certainly not a comfortable theater. Nietzche said that the Greeks put up white statues against the black abyss, in order to hide it. I, instead, topple them in order to reveal it . . . the tragedy of the modern spirit.

In toppling the white statues that hide the black abyss of the modern spirit, we court madness. And nowhere is that crucial moment more effectively argued than in Pirandello''s *Henry IV*.

In this play, Pirandello gives us a kaleidoscopic vision of a dead and deadening world such as Dante describes when — at the beginning of the *Commedia* — he looks back into the dark forest, his soul still running forward, trying to escape. Dante is rooted to the spot in a state of shock. We can only guess what might have happened at that moment when, in his weakened physical and spiritual condition he faces new terror in the three beasts that threaten to destroy him. *Henry IV* may be compared to that moment of shock and new awareness.

The protagonist, we soon learn, suffered a concussion and a complete loss of memory when he fell (or was pushed) from his horse as he rode as the Emperor Henry IV in a *mardi gras* pageant twenty years earlier. Embedded, as it were, in the role he had assumed for the occasion, he secluded himself in a mansion which he transformed into an 11th-century castle, with servants dressed to play retainers of the time. We discover, later in the play, that he had, in fact, regained his memory eight year earlier but decided to continue the fiction, thinking it was to late to re-enter a world that had passed him by.

That decision is put to a rough test by the intrusion of erstwhile friends who come with the idea of shocking him out of his amnesia. These include the Marchesa, his former fiancé, who rode with him in the pageant as Matilda of Tuscany; her daughter Frieda; Belcredi, Henry's old rival for the Marchesa's affections; a psychiatrist; and Henry's nephew, De Nolli. Their plan is to shock the "emperor" back into the present by producing double images, a series of superimposed masks, that will bridge the twenty-year gap. The Marchesa's daughter Frida, who bears a striking resemblance to her mother, dressed in the very same costume her mother wore at the *mardi gras* pageant twenty years earlier, will stand in the niche where a portrait hangs of the Marchesa at Frieda's age, in the identical costume. The Marchesa herself will stand nearby, in the same costume. De Nolli as Henry IV, will stand in the niche where a painting hangs of his uncle in the same 11th-century costume.

But Henry is perfectly sane now and intensely aware of what is going on; it is up to him to reveal and destroy the masks, one by one, and assume his own identity at last. Pirandello's protagonist argues his earlier decision with perfect lucidity and reason:

> I preferred to remain mad — since I found everything ready and at my disposal for this new exquisite fantasy. I would live it — this madness of mine — with the most lucid consciousness; and thus revenge myself on the brutality of a stone which had dented my head. The solitude — this solitude — squalid and empty as it appeared to me when I opened my eyes again — I determined to deck it out with all the colors and splendors of that far off day of carnival. . . .

In their effort to jolt Henry back into the present, however, the visitors have provoked a confrontation that destroys all possibility of realizing the end they had envisioned. Revealing the true state of things Henry takes the offensive:

> I would oblige all those who were around me to follow, by God, at my orders that jest of a day. I would make it become — for ever — no more a joke but a reality, the reality of a real madness; have all in masquerade, in the

throne room, and these my four secret counsellors; secret and, of course, traitors.

The traitors include Belcredi, the Marchesa's lover and Henry's old rival, the man who Henry is convinced pushed him from his horse and is responsible for all that followed. Now perfectly sane, Henry explains his role-playing and theirs:

> This dress, which is for me the evident masquerade, of which we are the involuntary puppets, when, without knowing it, we mask ourselves with that which we appear to be . . . that dress of theirs, this masquerade of theirs, of course, we must forgive it them, since they do not yet see it is identical with themselves. . . . You know, it is quite easy to get accustomed to it. One walks about as a tragic character, just as if it were nothing . . . in a room like this. . . . Look here, doctor! I remember a priest, certainly Irish, a nice looking priest, who was sleeping in the sun one November day, with his arm on the corner of the bench of a public garden. He was lost in the golden delight of the mild sunny air which must have seemed for him almost summery. One may be sure that in that moment he did not know any more that he was a priest, or even where he was. He was dreaming. . . . A little boy passed with a flower in his hand. He touched the priest with it here on the neck. I saw him open his laughing eyes, while his mouth smiled with the beauty of his dream. He was forgetful of everything. . . . But all at once, he pulled himself together and stretched out his priest's cassock; and there came back to his eyes the same seriousness which you have seen in mine; because the Irish priests defend the seriousness of their Catholic faith with the same zeal with which I defend the sacred rights of hereditary monarchy! I am cured, gentlemen; because I can act the madman to perfection here; and I do it very quietly, I'm only sorry for you that have to live your madness so agitatedly, without knowing it or seeing it.

Henry is whole again, but the others are still trapped in their illusions, more mad than he ever was. Henry finally accuses Belcredi of having pushed him off his horse on that fateful day, twenty years earlier;

and in the fray that follows, stabs his old enemy. Belcredi, is carried off, mortally wounded, and Henry is once again alone, forced to continue his fiction, trapped forever in his role as the mad Emperor.

Henry IV is also the *realization* or the *answer* to the dichotomy of stage and life, dramatized so effectively in the "theater plays." It is also a new threshold in the Pirandellian repertory: in it the stage and "real" life are fused, and role-playing is more than acting. Unlike the theater plays, this one runs, as it were, on a single track. And the "exorcism" it depicts goes beyond the fiction that has been put forward.

In his later plays (*Henry IV*, written in 1921, is still early in the repertory), Pirandello will elaborate in many different ways his "new idiom," but nowhere in such a memorable setting as that of *Henry IV*.

THE CREATIVE WILL

I

In his late novel, *Uno, nessuno e centomila* (*One, No One, and a Hundred Thousand*), Pirandello traces, through the main character, Moscarda, speaking in the first person, the breakdown of personality in a comic but metaphorically significant story of how the man tries to see himself as he "really" is. His wife asks him one day, had he ever noticed that his nose was a little crooked.? Moscarda of course, finds it difficult to check out for himself what his wife saw. At home, he tries mirrors; outside, he stops at store windows to study his reflection in the glass. To see what his wife saw, standing across from him, becomes an obsession until, finally, he enters an asylum, where he will be free to pursue the matter full-time.

His wife, his friends, the townspeople see in his obsession a kind of madness; and, in fact, Moscarda uses their response as a convenient excuse to move away from home, away from those distorted mirrored images of himself reflected in his relatives and friends.

Moscarda's "madness" is the culmination of a series of comic-absurd confrontations, paradoxes, dialectical reversals that are the signet mark of Pirandello's work. The novel is concentrated, fast-moving, dizzying in its effect, a *tour-de-force*, in a way. In its internal dialectic it is very similar to his first novel, *Il fù Mattia Pascal* (*The Late Mattia Pascal*), in which we have, already fully articulated, the same circling or spiraling toward the true self.

These two novels provide a framework for an examination of that typically "Absurd" dialectic which is the playwright's most innovative feature: the destruction of uncritical reality and the emergence of internal certainty, through the mirroring of self in endless reflections. At any given moment, we are and we are not. Most of us don't seek our true selves by leaving home and our jobs, as Moscarda does, or by assuming a new identity elsewhere, as Mattia Pascal does. These are extreme cases. But they give warning that an uncritical assumption as to who we are is a kind of death. The misleading notion that we are the image we find posited in the external world has to be abandoned. That image of an illusory solid *one* must be reduced to nothing, *no one*, before the *true integrated self* can emerge. And that true self is constantly changing, a hundred thousand masks, never the same from one moment to the next.

Mirror images come naturally and easily in such a context. They are especially effective in *One, No One, and a Hundred Thousand*, but we find them also in the plays. The most striking example is in *Right You Are!* Alone, after trying to convince his family and the other gossips who have assembled to find out the "truth" about their neighbor Signora Frola and her son-in-law Signor Ponza, one of the leading players, Laudisi, indulges in a dialogue with his mirror image, an exchange that is both comic and revealing.

> Ah, there you are! My dear man! — Which of us is mad, eh? Yes, I know: I say *you* are, and you point to *me*. — Come now, between us, we know each other well, we two! — The trouble is that others don't see you the way I do! And so, my dear fellow, what does that make you? For my part, here in front of you, I see myself, touch myself — you, as others see you, what are you? A ghost, my dear fellow, a ghost! — And yet, look at these madmen here! They ignore the ghost they carry with them, in themselves, and go running, bursting with curiosity, after the ghosts in others! And they really believe that it's different!

This confrontation is more than an aside. Laudisi is the embodiment of a dichotomy that remains unresolved. The mirror image is the moment of self-consciousness, the middle term of the Pirandellian equation. Laudisi is still *outside* himself in this clever dialogue with his ephemeral self, but he has also understood that his relatives and friends, pursuing an elusive truth in external "facts" are running further and further away from certainty.

The "facts" as presented by the intruders in *Six Characters in Search of an Author*, evoke a similar effort to objectify their moment of self-consciousness, their willful decision to externalize what is internal, to create their truth as immediate and eternal on a stage that is more than a stage. The attempt fails, of course, for those watching and listening are not prepared to accept the certainty the six characters embody. They have not gone through the same crucible. The willful assertion of the truth can have no meaning for those who have not gone through a similar experience.

There is something frightening, writes Georges Duhamel, about these six characters, who want us to know who they *really* are:

> Where are we? Beyond darkness? Beyond life, perhapa. Precisely that: all these characters are familiar to us; we recognize the profile, the gestures, the sound of the voice — they are all we know! And yet, we know nothing about them. We soon discover that they are "beyond," on the "other" side. And a kind of terror fills us. Just think: instead of two faces, they may turn out to have a hundred, a thousand.

The Father himself cues us in as to the masks we wear:

> Each of us thinks himself "one," but it's not true. He is "many," my friends, as "many" as there are possibilities in us. "One" with this fellow, "one" with that other. . . . And always under the illusion that we are "one and the same" for all, and always that same "one" we *think* we are, in all we do.

His desperate striving to communicate the certainty of what he has discovered about himself is a kind of madness. This obsession is reinforced at the end, when the entire family rush off, a falling into "darkness," their drama aborted, as it will always be, so long as they keep searching for an author who will find words for the certainty the others have not begun to address. They leave behind them a stage echoing with their passions, frustration, violence. Their agony seems to have reached beyond our sensibilities to that "other" side, where the stage is not an illusion but life itself. "What is for you people an illusion waiting to be shaped," the Father tells the actors,

> for us is our only reality. Not for us alone, mind you. Think about it. Can you tell me who you are? . . . . If *we* have no other reality beyond this illusion, you'd better look again at what you think is *your* reality, the one that you breathe and touch today, because — like yesterday's — it will turn out to be an illusion, tomorrow.

The actors (and the audience) are meant to see themselves somehow mirrored in the story told them by the Father or at least to acknowledge the strength of will that moves them. Actually, the circumstances of the story are only window dressing: the "fact" of incest is terrible, but even more terrible is the unfolding of that "fact" in the dramatic replay attempted.

In *Six Characters*, Pirandello has made a point of the impossibility of communicating the certainty of the will to others who have not gone through the experience, at the same time drawing us into a reality that reaches beyond the stage into our own consciousness of the contradictions we embody. No where else is this message more explicit than in this play, where the creative force of the will is shown on a stage inadequate to do it justice. At the same time, that stage gives body and voice to the contradictions we ourselves embody.

II

Pirandello found new and exciting ways to des‐ cribe the paradox of a "reality" that is not real until we have built it for ourselves. He did this not as a relativist (as some critics insist) but as a Socratic asses-

---

Part II first appeared under the title "Pirandello: Experience as the Expression of Will*," in* Forum Italicum, *Vol. VII, No. 3, September 1973, pp. 404-414. (Revised)*

sor of the world around us, forcing us to probe experience and make it a part of a conscious integrated *willful* whole. His characters often verge on madness in their emotional opposition to and revolt against the "facts" of life and the abstract values accepted by naive experience. Against "formal" acceptance of reality as "fact," he produces a dialectic of contradictory impulses. *Six Characters in Search of an Author*, *Right You Are!*, *Henry IV*, and even an early play like *Liolà*, are excellent examples of his concern for new dramatic forms to express the paradoxes in life, a new language that will sustain those paradoxes. This new vision of the theater will find extraordinary expression and variety in the "theater plays" and *Enrico IV*, but *Liolà* gives a strong signal of what is to come.

Pirandello is indeed, as Robert Brustein tells us, the "father of the contemporary theater," but he is also the father of "Theater of the Absurd" in his insistence on the fragmentation of dramatic action and the dissolution of character. His new breed of players, although individualized and finished dramatically, are unique in their obsession with inner life, their exploration of motives, emotions, and states of mind. They embody the dichotomy of the external image we automatically accept, by habit, and the internal multifaceted *persona* that waits to be discovered. They give voice to the process that redefines the world around us and leads to what is truly "real."

Pirandello was the first to formulate this new challenge with a clear understanding of its full implications for the stage. It wasn't experimentation that prompted him to sacrifice traditional realism. His new techniques were fully realized at the outset; emerging as the natural and therefore perfect expression of a new expanding stage that presented life as a struggle between rote acceptance and internal certainty.

There is nothing "cerebral" about Pirandello's approach. He brought into his plays, tangentially (and perhaps naively at times) subjects that fascinated him as, for example, Freudian psychology, but never as an end in itself, a fetish that had to be shared. He knew that allowing his own enthusiasm for certain subjects to take over the stage would compromise the action but if used properly could prove effective. His dramatic interests kept him from indulging in intellectual arguments. He never betrayed the dramatic core of his plays: man's painful self-confrontations, his self-probing for the infinite reflections of his true image.

To reach that true image of self, the world as we know it must be disassembled. "Facts" must be scrutinized with Socratic perseverance that either validates them internally, or rejects them. "Reality" thus redefined, is a dialectic of the will, shaping and reshaping human intentions into self-conscious completed deeds.

Such a premise forces new dramatic forms into being. Dramatic action is no longer unambiguous political, social, or critical statement. Theme, as traditionally understood, is hard to define. Dialectic replaces statement; and familiar realism becomes a question. Dramatic action turns into a kaleidoscopic experience, unsettling at first, but unerring in its implications. Language is no longer communication as we know it but a sifting through familiar words to find correspondences, echoes; to prod us into a new awareness of the limits of so-called reality, of the shifting of things familiar into an unknown world. Characterization as understood in the past gives way to an internal struggle to find the integral self. The protagonist does not change in any obvious way; he is transformed in the laser beam of a moment of crisis.

Instinct, revelation, doubt, confusion, assertion, denial all come into play in the process of turning inward for assurance and conviction. This dramatic impulse to find objective correlatives for the fluctuations of internal life produces *maschere nude*, naked masks — characters stripped of superficial "givens," made vulnerable in the exposure, but redeemed by the solid strength of conviction rooted in the will and the soul. What we have is not "reality vs illusion," whatever that means, but the *affirmation of the will* through a series of contradictions. The play is the effort to share that affirmation.

The dissolution of character on the modern stage is first portrayed in *Six Characters in Search of an Author*. In this extraordinary play, the six intruders walk on stage fully rendered in their *eternal moment*, much like Michelangelo "released" his David from the block of marble which contained him, potentially, in his perfect eternal posture. That posture tells the whole story, just as in Pirandello's play the one moment the characters are destined to replay *ad infinitum*, tells us everything we need to know about them. Anything else is gratuitous.

In the effort to communicate the eternal moment that dominates their lives, the six characters faced seemingly insurmountable obstacles. Their obsession is acknowledged only superficially by the "actors" (and the audience). Even a script provided by the Father is not enough to translate for others the experience that is *their* whole being. Nothing the actors do comes close to the perfection, the intensity of that eternal moment as the characters have lived it.

In their all-consuming purpose to strip away everything but the single moment of self-definition, the intruders dissolve as "characters" and assume postures and emotions that reveal the absolute nature of their commitment, as opposed to the transitory and superficial world of the acting troupe. The secret of the play lies in this single thrust of their being and the effort of their unswerving will to communicate what is, in effect, incommunicable by means of words alone.

In one of the scripted intermissions of *Each in His Own Way*, one of the critics discussing the pros and cons of the Pirandello play they are watching sums up his response with: "I feel as though I'm watching a mirror gone crazy." Confusion, here as elsewhere, is in fact an essential term in Pirandello's dramatic equation. It is not meant to be the answer to anything.

He uses it, like a good doctor, to effect a cure, to bring us to self-awareness and internal resolution. Confusion helps to dispel the illusion of the ready-made shape of things.

The ultimate paradox, of course, is that Pirandello undermines the traditional stage, not to destroy it but to restructure it to serve his purpose. The techniques he introduces are integral and therefore effective. In this lies his genius: that he remained true to the exigencies of the theater as a distinct form of art while infusing it with all the novelty and immediacy of an existential "happening," taking down the barrier between the stage and the audience in the process.

THE PSYCHOLOGY OF THE ALIENATED: THE WOMEN IN PIRANDELLO'S PLAYS

In his excellent introduction to the translation of Prometheus Bound, Professor C. J. Herington of Yale reminds us that in his moment of greatest agony, pinned to a rock of perpetual pain, Prometheus nevertheless enjoys a great advantage over the Olympian gods as well as over his fellow Titans: Earth-Gaea, the aged grandmother of the divine dynasty which rules Olympus, has given him the secret of what may ultimately destroy Zeus. Mother Earth "knows," as Herington puts it,

> she has an awareness of destiny, of the way things really are, that is denied even the highest male gods, Guranos, Kronos, and Zeus himself.

There is another sort of woman in Prometheus' life at this first glimmer of the birth of dramatic art. As Hesiod, that "deplorably antifeminist poet," tells us, the immediate consequence of the "sin" committed by Prometheus was that sorry business evoked by the mere mention of "Pandora." We know the unqualified disaster that name automatically calls up. Hesiod's account parallels that of the Bible, where Eve's sin is redeemed by Mary's grace. Hesiod does not redeem Pandora himself, but Aeschylus does. Io, the lovely girl raped by Zeus, will produce among her progeny, Hercules, who will thwart what appears to be the will of Zeus by releasing Prometheus. All of this is central to the *Prometheus Bound* of Aeschylus, in which the prophecy of Mother Earth to Prometheus looms large. The most importance characters in that play, besides Prometheus himself, are Io and the chorus of women who represent the daughters of Ocean.

A very brief version of this paper was delivered at a Modern Language Association convention early in the seventies. The present essay has been much enlarged.

These examples from the dawn of mythology remind us of the oscillating extremes of acceptance and rejection which are the history of women as their chauvinist critics record it. The tradition of the Greeks and Jews furnish us with a clear picture of the unique adaptability of women in all kinds of situations, their special aptitudes and qualities, bordering often on the prophetic, and a vivid reminder that their firm determination in joy and suffering gives them a more demanding role in life but also a much greater potential for heroic and dramatic self-realization. From the beginning of literary expression, women who succeed have been represented as doing so against tremendous odds, and a corollary appears to be that, in success, they often prove themselves better than men, for the obstacles in their path are greater.

In writing this, I recalled a TV program I hosted for NBC back in the early seventies, "Successful Women, Before, During and After Women's Lib." My guests were Marion Stephenson, first woman Vice-President of NBC; Margaret Rumbarger, Executive Secretary of the American Association of University Women, Ponchitta Pierce of Channel 7; Kathleen Carroll, film critic for *The Daily News*, and Margaret Kelly, Vice-President of St. John's University in New York. One dominant idea emerged in these interviews: that a woman must ultimately compete with men on the same level, right to the top, through intense training, above average preparation, tremendous stamina, extraordinary competence, and a profound self-knowledge based on constant self-evaluation; and that, if successful, she must continue to be devastatingly competitive. At the other end of the spectrum, the panel agreed that women must act together as a pressure group to insure public recognition and practical changes in response to their demands for what is after all their birthright: to be treated in the same way and given the same opportunities as men.

The Psalmist might have said in the original version before the chauvinists censured it: "What is woman that thou are mindful of her?" Hamlet exclaims: "What a piece of work is man" but then adds, in a less idealistic context: "Man delight me not; no, nor woman neither."

Aeschylus was perhaps the first to give arresting dramatic expression to the special qualities displayed by women, but literature is full of similar examples. Besides the divinely-inspired Antigone, we have among the Greeks the determined Medea, the far-seeing Cassadra. They have negative counterparts, needless to say, and we must not shy away from making true and proper distinctions or else we might seem foolish in the eyes of the rest of the world. But at their best, women like Antigone, Medea, Ophelia, Desdemona, Cleopatra, even Lady Macbeth; or if we turn to modern drama, women like Tennessee Williams' Blanche or Laura, or those in many of Edward Albee's plays,[1] represent an ideal which is more demanding than anything comparable in the male world. Such women are isolated, struggle alone in a man's world and emerge victorious even in the face of madness and death. They echo in their instinctive expression of right and wrong, in their unswerving commitment to what they know to be true, the voice of Mother Earth.

Nowhere in the history of modern dramatic literature has this notion been explored artistically with so many variants and in so many different contexts as in the plays (and fiction) of Luigi Pirandello. The women he depicts are often destroyed, humbled and ostracized because of their instinctive leap to what is right and true. They are forced into decisions that threaten their entire world; or adjust to a male-dominated situation at tremendous personal expense. They are heroic in their resignation and in their headlong flight to destruction for the sake of what is right. Their commitment is inspiring: their conviction often rejects common sense and defies argument.

Pirandello, who gave such powerful voice to such women and, through them, speaks to us still, acknowledged his own personal confrontation with the woman who was his partner in life and who shaped and clarified, in that painful union, his understanding of women.

> One who lives and suffers the torment of a person one loves cannot look on at a distance. . . . But still, watching how life was being transformed in the soul of my poor wife enabled me to grasp, later, in my creations, the psychology of the alienated. . . . . Life is without logic, without form. That's why I am convinced that those who are crazy come closer to the meaning of life. (*My translation*)
>
> [Chi soffre e vive il tormento di una persona che si ama non a modo di studiare. . . . Ma certo il vedere come si trasformava la vita nello spirito della mia povera compagna, mi potè dare l'avvertimanto a sentire, poi, nella creazione, la psicologia degli alienati. . . . La vita è informa e illogica. Perciò io credo che i pazzi siano piñ vicini alla vita.][2]

His wife Antonietta had started showing symptoms of some kind of psychological disorder early in their marriage. Three children did not improve the situation. The illness grew worse; when she became violent — jealous of her own daughter and difficult to control, Pirandello had her committed. She lived on for many years, in a world of her own. Watching her deterioration, her obsessions grow, Pirandello came to know first-hand about madness — more perhaps than he himself was willing to admit. There can be no doubt that it was through observation of a woman in the throes of a losing battle with an alien world that Pirandello came to understand and portray the creative madness of some of his best characters.

The outstanding example is, of course, not a woman but the "mad" emperor who goes by the name of Henry IV. But the women in Pirandello's repertory bring conflicts into focus in a number of ways that deserve to be examined. We find them often in situations that lead to intense emotional reactions; situations that threaten the very foundation of their world. He depicts them struggling against forces far greater than their own internal resources but with an instinctive commitment that belies the obvious imbalance. His women range from Eves to Beatrices; and in his three late "myth" plays, *The New Colony* (*La nuova colonia*), *Lazarus* (*Lazzaro*), and *The Mountain Giants* (*I Giganti della montagna*), he depicts woman as something of an icon, a symbol: the fertile mother of mankind's ultimate salvation — not through art, not through politics, not through religion, but through a resurrected faith in life. They are the harbingers of hope and optimism, the inspiration behind art itself.

Pirandello opens the Preface to his collected plays, *Maschere nude*, with a spirited description of "an exceptionally quick little servant maid" ("una servetta sveltissima"), who comes and goes as she pleases, her moods unpredictable, who likes to dress in black, at times eccentrically, and carries in her pocket a bright red cap with bells, which she plops on her head as she runs out.

> And she amuses herself by bringing into the house, so I can work them into my short stories, novels, and plays, the most unhappy people in the world, men women, children caught up in strange circumstances from which they can no longer find release; frustrated in their plans, cheated of their hopes; and, in a word, dealing with whom often takes a tremendous effort.
>
> [E si diverte a portarmi in casa, perchè io ne tragga novelle e romanzi e commedie, la gente più scontenta del mondo, uomini, donne, ragazzi, avvolti in casi strani da cui non trovan più modo di uscire; contrariati nei loro disegni; frodati nelle loro speranze; e coi quali insomma è spesso veramente una gran pena trattare.]

That little servant girl is *Fantasia*, Pirandello tells us, the creative imagination that follows her own whims and forces herself on the artist, who, yielding to her, gives birth to dramatic characters. "And so the artist, in his lifetime," Pirandello elaborates,

> draws into himself many germs of life, and he can never

say how or why, at a certain moment one of those crucial germs finds its way into the imagination, to become itself a living creature on a plane of life far above our daily, unpredictable existence.

[Così un artista, vivendo, accoglie in se tanti getmi della vita, e non può mai dire come e perchè, in un certo momento, uno di questi germi vitali gli si inserisca nella fantasia per divenire anch'esso una creatura viva in un piano di vita superiore alla volubile esistenza quotidiana.]

Fantasy is responsible for bringing those six characters "into the house," into Pirandello's fertile brain, forcing him to deal with them.

When he does, it is a woman, the Mother, who shows resignation and quiet acceptance, speaking only when her family is threatened or to correct the misunderstandings brought on by The Father in his effort to communicate the urgency and importance of the story that he feels must somehow be transmitted to others. It is The Mother who brings things into focus when she insists that what The Father describes as having already taken place is in fact happening right then and there,

> it is happening now, it is happening always. My torment is not over, sir; I am alive and here, always, in every moment of my torment that renews itself always, real and present.

> [no, avviene ora, avviene sempre. Il mio strazio non è finito, signore! Io sono viva e presente, sempre, in ogni momento del mio strazio, che si rinnova vivo e presente sempre.]

The Mother accepts her suffering as a present reality, never to be assuaged. She is obviously special in Pirandello's eyes. When the six first appear, the author's stage directions recommend that they be masked to show the emotion each represents: remorse for The Father, revenge for Step-Daughter, disdain for the Son, and suffering for The Mother. But whereas a single word suffices for the others, he describes. The

Mother's mask in some detail:

> ... *suffering* for the Mother with fixed wax eyes, visible in the dark shadows under her eyes and on her cheeks, such as are seen in the sculptures and paintings of the *Mater dolorosa* found in the churches.
>
> [... il *dolore* per la Madre con fisse lacrime di cera, nel livido delle occhiaje e lungo le gote, come si vedono nelle immagini scolpite e dipinte della *Mater dolorosa* nelle chiese.]

Her role, she herself insists, is a special one. Her daughter is there as a *show* of herself, not really as she, The Mother, is there.

> If I see her before me now, it is solely for this, only for this, always, always to renew in me always, alive and present, the torment that I have suffered for her also.
>
> [Se ora io me la vedo qua è ancora per questo, solo per questo, sempre, sempre per rinvigorarmi sempre, vivo e presente, lo strazio che ho sofferto anche per lei,]

Pirandello does not give The Mother occasion to respond to the efforts of an actress to play her part, to hold a mirror up to her. Unlike Step-Daughter, she has no desire to dramatize her suffering. Step-Daughter, on the other hand, is eager to enact the moment when she almost gave herself to a man who, as it turned out, was her mother's husband. She has in her Medea's lust for revenge, Antigone's loyalty to family, the irrational urge to punish, to lay bare The Father's sins, to protect her mother. The bond between the two women is strong. It is significant (as well as ironic) that The Mother — employed by Madame Pace to make hats — unaware that the store is a front for a brothel — should be the one to stumble upon and abort what would have been considered incest. That one action, her only contribution to the re-enactment, unravels the hidden truth. It is she who recognizes the Man who is about to have sex with Step-Daughter as her husband.

In *Each in His Own Way* (*Ciascuno a suo modo*) it is again a woman who brings the action to a climax with her emotional outbursts, on and "off" the stage, in a multi-level theater experience. On stage, Delia Morello is playing the part of Amelia Morena, who has come to see just how far the author (Pirandello) has gone in portraying her alleged infedelity, a scandal that has ostracized her socially and drove her fiance to suicide. Morena dominates the "Interludes" or intermissions, which are part of the script. When she comes face to face with her lover, who is also in the theater, hoping to see her and talk to her, in spite of efforts by friends on both sides to keep them apart, she realizes that it is useless to try to escape him: they are forever bound by what they have done. With that realization, they rush off into the darkness together, leaving behind stunned spectators and a new source of sordid gossip. The actors in the stage play, unwilling to compete with that kind of drama, announce that they will not continue with their performance that evening because of all the mayhem caused by the two lovers.

In *Tonight We Improvise*, the vulnerability and suffering of the woman is powerfully drawn in the character of Mommina, the abused wife who is kept a virtual prisoner in her own home by a jealous husband. The setting here is the closed rigorous society which is the background for so many of Pirandello's plays, short stories, and novels. The actress playing Mommina is so devastated (or so much "into" her role) that at a certain moment she collapses and faints, bringing the other actors out of their parts to cluster around her, thinking she has been taken ill.

The critic Ferdinando Virdia sees in this third "theater play" the transition from a local scenario to a larger one:

> . . . *Tonight We Improvise* is the text that clearly marks the dividing line between the Sicilian Pirandello and the "European" Pirandello. . . . the theme of jealousy, of the bitter and raging jealousy of the past, the myth of honor and of the past, horribly endured personally by the author in his family life, is one of the :lines: of a certain tragic and Pirandellian "humoristic" Sicilianism.

In this context, the character of Mommina is typical of a feminine condition that is locked in its ancient solitude, at the "daily mercy of a world without music, waiting for infinite musical possibilities," in Giacomo De Benedetti's astute definition.

[... Questa sera si recita a soggetto è il testo che segna nettamenta il punto di sutura tra il Pirandello siciliano e il Pirandello "europeao," . . . il tema della gelosia, dell'amara e furente gelosia del passato, il mito dell'onore e del passato, atrocemente sofferto di persona dallo sccrittore nella sua vita familiare, è una delle "corde" di un certo tragico e pirandellianamente "umoristico" sicilianismo. Il personaggio di Mommina è in questo senso esemplare di una condizione femminile chiusa nella sua antica solitudine, nel servaggio di un mondo senza musica, sospeso ad una infinita possibilità musicale," secondo l'acutissima definizaione di Giacomo De Benedetti.]

Mommina is indeed locked in a long-suffering situation in a world without music or anything that lifts the soul. Virdia goes on to compare Mommina to the protagonist of Pirandello's early novel, *L'esclusa (The Outcast)*, where this theme is rendered most powerfully.

In a way Mommina is a younger sister of Marta Ajala, the protagonist of *The Outcast*, she too hanging on the thread of suspicion, of a marriage full of anguish (which in the novel was also a collective anguish, the neurosis of a society, desperate and obsessive but also cruel and disdainful, a meek and suffering victim whose only refuge is in the world that tortures and kills her).

[Mommina à in un certo senso una sorella minore di Marta Ajala, la protagonista del *L'esclusa*, anch'essa sospesa sul filo del sospetto, di un'angoscia maritale (che nel romanzo era anche angoscia colletiva, la neurosi di una società, disperata e ossessiva, ma anche crudele e sprezzante, vittima mite e dolorosa, il cui unico refugio à nel mondo che la strazia e l'uccide).]

Mommina's home life is much like Pirandello's, only in the play the roles are reversed: it is the husband who is mad with jealousy, not the wife.

Pirandello understands his time and place. His compassion extends easily to the women who inhabit his world, for they had even fewer options open to them than the men, restricted forever to a closed society of long-standing prejudices and taboos. Antonietta's mother had died in childbirth because she would not let herself be seen by a doctor. Her father, Calogero Portolano, instructed the women of the house never to open the shutters beyond a prescribed point; and it was said that he would not buy a certain house because it had no bars at the window — a necessary obstruction to keep the women from leaning out and be seen by people below.

The terrible results of jealousy, in such a society, of women exploited and used, are depicted again and again in Pirandello's works. In *Six Characters* the central event is incest, caught in time and prevented, but the horror of which lingers on and is doomed to be replayed forever. (Bad enough, but not nearly as bad as the real-life situation, in which Antonietta accused her own daughter of luring her father into incest. The girl tried to commit suicide as a result, saved only by inexperience. Nonetheless, she had to be sent away to live with an aunt, because Antonietta was firm: "Either she goes, or I go." ["Fuori lei, o fuori io."])

There is something of Pirandello's genuine compassion and continued love for Antonietta in The Father's account of the emptiness that closed in on him after he had sent The Mother away.

> Once she was gone, my house suddenly was empty. She was my incubus, but she had filled the place! Alone, I found myself moving about in those rooms like a fly without a head.
>
> [La mia casa, andata via lei, mi provò subito vuota. Era il mio incubo, ma me la riempiva! Solo, mi ritrovai per le stanze come una mosca sensa capo.]

What we can be sure of is that he was able, with the

The Psychology of the Alienated: The Women / 137

help of his whimsical *Fantasia*, to give his own personal incubus the distance and release of art.

There is compassion, understanding and a kind of redemption in his portrayal of the unfulfilled wife in the one-act play, *At the Exit (All'uscite)*. Here we find half-baked "ghosts" waiting for their one great wish to be granted before they can be released from all earthly ties. Fat Man (the woman's husband), recently expired, waits for his one wish to be realized: to see his wife weep instead of laughing hysterically all the time. She enters, having just been killed by her lover, laughing and dancing, just as her husband remembers her; but at the sight of a cart going by with a little boy sitting in the back, she bursts into tears and runs after it, reaching out for the child she never had and will never have. As her husband describes her: "She was never happy, not even with her lover, nothing, no one could make her happy." She herself recognizes her terrible longings:

> I had hoped, I had hoped that that last kiss finally, oh God, would have brought the warmth that my anguished body always, and always in vain yearned for, and that with that warmth I might now live again, get well.
>
> [Sperai, sperai che quell'ultimo bacio finalmente, oh Dio, mi avesse dato il calore che le mie viscere esasperate hanno sempre, e sempre invano, bramato, e che con quel caldo ora potessi rivivere, guarire.]

When she runs off weeping, the husband disappears, his last wish granted. His wife, we have to believe, will never get over her restlessness and longing. Pirandello abandons her to her eternal limbo of desire.

Mita, in Pirandello's early masterpiece *Liolà*. is one of the earliest and youngest of Pirandello's "trapped" women. A poor servant girl, she has been forced to marry Uncle Simone, a rich old man who needs an heir. Mita and Liolà are childhood sweethearts who realize they can have no future together; they are too poor to marry and have wisely kept a certain distance. Mita is the only means of support for her widowed mother; Liolà supports his own widowed mother as well as the bastards he has fathered with village girls who were irresistibly drawn to the handsome, happy-go-lucky young man.

Uncle Simone will not admit he is unable to make Mita pregnant (just as he was unable to make his first wife pregnant, in their many years together). Angry and frustrated at Mita's inability to produce an heir, he accepts a bizarre offer by another village girl, Tuzza, who is pregnant with Liolà's child. Uncle Simone agrees to take Tuzza's child and claim it as his own — neither overly concerned about the scandal their action will give rise to. When Liolà hears of this, he is furious and works out a plan to thwart Tuzza's greed and to make sure she doesn't establish herself as a permanent fixture in Uncle Simone's house. He tells Mita in no uncertain terms that she must produce the heir, and in the same way that Tuzza did. The girl is shocked; her entire world is threatened by the suggestion, all the values she holds dear are put to an awesome test. But Liolà is convincing. His argument is foolproof, inspired even. He drives on mercilessly. Are we to wait for another virgin birth? he asks bluntly. Tuzza will rule in your own house once her bastard has been installed as Uncle Simone's heir. Is that how you want to live out the rest of your life? Your husband is ready to go along with Tuzza's plan; but think how quickly he will abandon it, once he learns that you, his wife, have become pregnant at last. Who will dare suggest that it is not his child you carry! Whatever rumors may arise will quickly dissipate, especially since he has never admitted that the fault is his. He will never doubt the child is his.

Liolà's strategy is a practical solution that will save the day. Tuzza, in spite of her cunning and shrewdness, will be turned away, as she deserves, and Mita will never have to worry about losing her place and status in her own home. This Machiavellian solution[3] has nothing to do with lust or sexual gratification. Liolà loves Mita but has always been proper and respectful with her, careful not to compromise her in any way; his only purpose is to protect her and punish Tuzza, whose arrogant proposition has forced his hand. His own pride too demands satisfaction. Mita eventually agrees. In the end, everyone will get what he or she wants without making waves.

In *Right You Are (If You Think So)* (*Così é [se vi pare]*), Councilman Agazzi, Signore Ponza's new employer, has called the man in, ostensibly to explain the unusual living arrangements he has made for himself and his wife and for his mother-in-law, Signora Frola, arrangements that have generated a good deal of gossip. But before Ponza has a chance to do so, Signora Frola pays a "courtesy" protocol call on the Agazzis, eager to explain that Signore Ponza is under the delusion that his wife, her daughter, has died and that he married again, but someone else. Signora Frola tells them that her daughter had been ill but recovered and was returned to her husband; but he refused to acknowledge her until they went through a mock ceremony, as though he were marrying someone else. Signora Frola has accepted Ponza's strange behavior to spare him further grief. He is, she goes on, kindness itself but overly protective of his wife and will not allow even Signora Frola to get too close to her. He has settled her, Signora Frola, in this very building just down the hall from the Aguzzis; while he and his wife rent an apartment in a humble walk-up on the edge of town. Signora Frola is allowed to visit her daughter but forbidden to climb up to be with her. They exchange notes by means of a basket that is lowered and raised as needed.

The Agazzis and the friends who've assembled for the occasion, are shocked. Ponza enters soon after and with a very different story. He tells his employer that he is protecting his mother-in-law, who believes his second wife to be her dead daughter. To make sure the two women never come face to face, he worked out the living arrangements that are causing so much gossip. He knows what poor Signora Frola is saying about him, but it's harmless enough and keeps her from succumbing again to the depression that almost destroyed her when her daughter died. Her thinking the girl recovered and is now back living with him is a small price to pay for Signora Frola's peace of mind.

These conflicting accounts force Agazzi to ask Signore Ponza to produce his wife. Surely she can tell them who she is! But when the woman arrives, heavily veiled, her enigmatic reply to the obvious question brings the play to a strange close: she is her mother's daughter and her husband's second wife. To those who do not understand the paradox she embodies, there can be no solution, no "truth."

Is that a straight answer? No, of course not. There can be no straight answer until we translate objective "facts" into the immediacy of intuitive certainty and conviction.

In his last three plays, another kind of "trilogy," Pirandello lays upon the women the immense task of illuminating, explaining, and mastering the large questions about existence. In these late plays, he asserts the intrinsic value of life through women who are outcasts in one way of another: La Spera (Hope) in *The New Colony (La nuova colonia)* is a rehabilitated prostitute. Sara in *Lazarus (Lazzaro)* has abandoned her husband and two children and gone to live with one of the hired hands on her husband's estate, raising a new family with him. Ilse in *The Mountain Giants (I Giganti della montagna)* destroys her marriage and her theatrical company because of her attachment to the memory of a young poet who died, leaving her a dramatic script on which she now lavishes all the passion and love she denied its author while he lived.

All three women have defied conventions; all three have asserted their independence; all three have paid heavily for their actions. Pirandello boldly justifies their behavior as a means toward personal redemption and greater perception, a means of redefining existing values. Without undermining family, religion, or social structures, he tests the notion of fallen nature against the demands of the soul. It is the women who shed light on the inner self, redefining the old values and asserting them in the illumination that comes with self-knowledge and personal faith.

In *The New Colony*, La Spera — despised, ill-treated, insulted, even by the common thieves and low-life characters around her — convinces the father of her infant son to start a new life on a deserted island away from the world that has almost destroyed them both. He, in turn, convinces his cronies to join him and sets down rules for the new settlement. For a while, they find refuge and peace in their ideal community, where the strength of the woman prevails. Her purpose and determination keep others in line; but after a while, jealousies crop up, old lusts surface, the world they had left behind overtakes the new colonists in their new Eden. La Spera is reduced once again to her former degraded position. Strife of every sort breaks out and new vices surface. The men become more vicious than before, La Spera tries desperately to save at least her child's father from sinking back into his old criminal ways but fails. Finally, the island itself begins to sink into the sea, as though responding to all the ugly things that have happened on it, taking with it all its inhabitants except La Spera, who has sought the high ground with her child in her arms.

The metaphor is transparent enough, if we want to see one in all this. The literal reading is simple enough: La Spera's will has not faltered; her conviction and strength have freed her from the bondage of external pressures and vain attractions, from the world's prejudices.

In *Lazarus*, the political lesson becomes a religious epiphany. Here too it is a woman who succeeds in "converting" others to the true meaning of life and love. Sara has pitted herself against her husband and children, destroying her family in order to start a new life with another man and raising a new family outside the bonds of marriage. She was driven to it, we learn, by her husband's cruel decision to place their two children, Lia and Lucio, in the care of others — the boy with priests, the girl with nuns. Lucio had taken on the habit of a seminarian, out of obedience and fear. The little girl, without her mother's love to sustain her, grew ill and was brought back to her parents' house an invalid. Realizing that her children were being destroyed by their father's rigorous demands, Sara had left her home and taken refuge in one of the tiny dwellings on the estate. She soon found the love and compassion her husband could not give her in the farmer-caretaker, Arcodipane (literally: "ark of bread").

When the play opens, Lucio has left the seminary to return to his mother, having come to share and identify with her beliefs. He now sees in her dedication to life an attitude much holier than his father's insistence on formal piety. By the end of the play, he has gained new insight and compassion but takes on again the habit of the seminarian in order to help save his father, who having been brought back to life after what appeared to be a fatal accident and not remembering anything, has lost his faith. The miracle of life is underscored at the very end, when the little girl gets out of her wheelchair and walks to her mother without help. Sara, like the enlightened Beatrice, never wavers. In her, Pirandello embodies the religious intuition that makes life itself an act of faith. For Sara, God is truly love, and to betray that love is to betray the world He created. She brings home the lesson that insight comes only through acceptance of the gift of love. The conventions of unexamined and thoughtless piety, necessary at first, can only do damage if not replaced with the faith dictated by the unerring soul.

In showing us the emptiness of habit and rote behavior, Pirandello is not attacking religious custom and practice. He is too intelligent to indulge in simplistic attacks on religion or anything else. He has no intention of undermining true religious belief. Sara simply triggers an examination of conscience, forcing a re-assessment of large mysteries, as a necessary step toward true understanding.

Sara has led others into accepting God in life and in nature; Ilse, in *The Mountain Giants*, tries to lead others into the exalted experience of inspired drama. Almost beside herself with grief at the loss of the young poet whose love she had denied him in life, she has dedicated herself to promoting the great work he has left behind. Together with her husband and the members of her acting company, she has been traveling from place to place in search not of an author but of an audience. The magic villa of the mysterious Cotrone becomes their temporary home, but the master of the villa explains that they must not try to perform the poet's work outside the walls of the estate. Only within those walls, among those who are ready to accept it, will the drama effectively come alive. Under Cotrone's magic spell, puppets are transformed into living creatures.

Ilse cannot accept the restrictions Cotrone has imposed. She insists that the world must be made aware of the power of the dead poet's art and insists on performing his work before the mountain folk, where their masters, the giants of our industrial society, hold sway. These have finally given her permission to stage the work for their people. But the play does not go down too well with the vulgar crowd who have come to be entertained. Sensing the contempt of the troupe, the crowd rise up in a frenzy of frustration and Ilse is killed.

When she had first declared her intention to put on the play outside the villa, a member of her troupe had commented:

One must never go against what the heart commands!

[Non si deve andar mai contro a ciò che il cuore commanda!]

It's not that simple, of course. Cotrone, the master magician, the puppet-master, is more perceptive in his response to Ilse's decision:

> Poor work of art! Just as the poet did not win her love, so will his work not win public acclaim.
>
> [Povera opera! Come il poeta non ebbe da lei l'amore, così l'opera non avrà dagli uomini la gloria.]

Cotrone is prophetic, but he cannot interfere with destiny. Ilse's insistence that the whole world must be made to admire her poet's work is turned into action and must run its course. When the experiment fails, the bereaved husband cries out that his wife's death marks the death of art. Cotrone corrects him:

> It's not that Poetry has been rejected, but only this: that the poor fanatical slaves of life, in whom today the spirit does not speak but may yet speak one day, have innocently routed, like rebellious puppets, the fanatical slaves of Art, who don't know how to speak to men because they have excluded themselves from life, but not so completely as to find satisfaction only in their own dreams; daring, rather, to impose them on those with other business to attend to besides indulging in such things.
>
> [Non è che la Poesia sia stata rifiutata, ma solo questo: che i poveri servi fanatici della vita, in cui oggi lo spirito non parla, ma potrà pur sempre parlare un giorno, hanno innocentemente rotto, come fantocci ribelli, i servi fanatici dell"Arte, che non sanno parlare agli uomini perchè si sono esclusi dalla vita, ma non tanto poi da appagarsi soltanto di proprii sogni, anzi pretendendo di imporli a chi ha altro da fare, che creder in essi.]

Cotrone spells out the tragic dimension of the confrontation Ilse has brought about. In so doing, he defines with candor and clarity the limits of both the work of art and the audience. The world, as in the other two plays, demands its due and will not be rejected easily.

In this, as in the other two "myth" plays, and in

THE PSYCHOLOGY OF THE ALIENATED: THE WOMEN

many of the earlier plays as well, Pirandello sustains the exalted ideals of the inspired few, who reach up higher than most, even at the expense of communal values. Throughout, women lead the way to greater understanding; but in these late plays, they emerge as embodiments of the most exalted ideals.

NOTES

1. For a detailed discussion of Edward Albee's plays, see Anne Paolucci: *From Tension to Tonic: The Plays of Edward Albee* (Southern Illinois University Press, Carbondale, Illinois, 1972, 1973; Griffon House Publications, New York, 2000) and *Edward Albee (The Later Plays)* (Griffon House Publications, New York, 2009).

2. See Luigi Pirandello, *Maschere nude* II Volumi (Arnoldo Mondadori Editori, 1958/1965). All quotations from the plays are from this edition. English translations are my own.

3. See, "Pirandello's *Liolà* and Machiavelli's *Mandragola*" later in this volume.

PART THREE
COMPARATIVE STUDIES

The New York Times
Sunday, March 27, 1994

The City

QU Section 13

Test Your Literary I.Q.: Level 1

Each of these writers is the hero, or heroine, of a literary society in New York. Read the clues and guess who they are.

By CONSTANCE L. HAYS

RONALD WEITZ spends his days in Brooklyn, overseeing a squad of city social workers who try to find help for cocaine-addicted babies.

But every few weeks he takes up a well-worn paperback, tones up his self-taught brogue and joins two dozen other New Yorkers to plumb the richly double-entendre'd depths of "Finnegans Wake." They read, reread and try to filter meaning from a few pages at a time. Three years beyond "Riverrun," they are still only 447 pages deep.

Ask Mr. Weitz to explain the fascination, and he settles for the simplest possible terms. "Joyce," he says, "has always appealed to me, for some reason or another."

Call it weird or escapist or write it off to the usual urban quest for identity. But across New York, literary societies are flourishing, focused on everything from children's books to murder mysteries to the fusty niceties of Victorian England. There is a group for fans of Anthony Trollope and another devoted to Mark Twain, one for Luigi Pirandello, another dedicated to C. S. Lewis, and several that study the "canon" of Sherlock Holmes.

Culver Pictures
6. A woman of sensibility

Associated Press, 1939
1. Elementary

2. Ghostwriter

Berenice Abbott
7. "Stephen Hero"

Your Literary I.Q.: Level 2

Pioneer Press, 1925
The feminist muse of Mankato, Minn.

5. How They Lived Then

1947
8. Archie Goodwin's Samuel Johnson

Bruni Foto Agencia, 1930
3. One playwright in search of an I.D.

Feeling smug?
For Level 2,
Read on.

Still feeling smug?
Answers ⟶

Pirandello's *Liolà* and Machiavelli's *Mandragola*

In spite of its simple construction, *Liolà* already contains many of the complexities of Pirandello later plays, claiming a place in his repertory similar to that of *Julius Caesar* in the evolution of Shakespeare's dramatic art or *The Zoo Story* in that of Edward Albee's. Its simplicity, as in Shakespeare's play and Albee's, is deceptive, however, for this unsophisticated early "naturalistic" work soon reveals itself as the author's first masterful attempt to explore what will be his signature as a playwright and novelist: the paradox of reality.

Liolà (1916) signals in many ways Pirandello's new approach to the stage. Set against the realistic background of his native Agrigento and with perfectly recognizable characters shown struggling against oppressive forces, he depicts a situation where rigorous conventions are sorely tested as the familiar vectors of greed, self-interest, and self-deception are worked into an intricate web of stunning and unexpected intrigue. In the process, traditional values are turned upside down as present and immediate events work their way to the completed deed, action is reconstituted right side up in the light of an irrefutable logic, at once consistent and bizarre.

Madness, grief, and self-recrimination are there only potentially. *Liolà* seems almost a light comedy compared with some of the later plays. Pirandello, in fact, called it "a country comedy," but the play contains the seeds of tragedy. Romantic love is illusory, an impossible dream in the kind of harsh environment of a rigorous, closed society. Like the seductive episode

---

First appeared in Comparative Literature Studies, *Vol. IX. No. 1, March 1972, pp. 44-56. (Revised)*

of Paolo and Francesca in the darkness of Dante's Hell, *Liolà* lulls us into a willing suspension of moral judgment in a setting reminiscent of the pastoral charm of Boccaccio's *Ninfale fiesolano*. Circumstances challenge conventional "morality" and demand a different kind of virtue. *Libido* is very subtly turned into *licito* (to use Dante's terse expression in describing Semiramis) by an act of faith dictated by personal conviction but relevant also in a large way, beyond the immediate circumstances. On the surface *Liolà* is indeed a "country comedy," but it soon becomes evident that it is really an emotional windstorm about self-interest, envy, hatred, cunning and deceit. It is not love that conquerors all but, paradoxically, those emotions that man's fallen nature finds hard to resist and that can be described in one word: selfishness.

The play is clearly a "first"; but it also enjoys with two other early plays the curious distinction of having been written originally in the dialect of Agrigento and performed — at the author's express request — in that dialect. (Pirandello took care to distinguish the genuine country vernacular which he used from the *dialetto borghese*, which was — according to him — a diluted form of Sicilian).

Liolà, the "hero," is, according to the author himself, a kind of sun-inebriated deity, a pagan god, who comes and goes: here one moment (lì). there the next (là). He emerges as a combination Pan and Dionysius in a Christian setting — the god of song and love seen against the compelling backdrop of religious taboos. The very names of the protagonists suggest a strange contrapuntal play of Biblical and mythological echoes: Ninfa, Croce, Mita (the meek one?) One might even argue with a certain amount of success that the play is a subtle parody of Christian values. The climax — the scene between Mita and Liolà, the night of Zio Simone's acknowledgement that the child fathered by Liolà, and carried by the village girl Tuzza will be raised as his own — contains what can only be described as ironic references to the Virgin birth.

The effect of this motif woven into the setting of a romantic innocent love recalls, by way of contrast, Machiavelli's dramatic masterpiece, *Mandragola*.[1] Pirandello, we know, considered the play one of the great works of Italian literature and — although we cannot prove Pirandello's intention — it may not be far-fetched to suggest that Machiavelli's play was the direct inspiration for *Liolà*. An examination of the two works strengthens that conclusion, and, of special interest to us here, it dramatizes the importance of Pirandello's new focus.

The ultimate source for both plays is, of course, the classic historical account of Livy's *Rape of Lucrece* — stripped, in the two later versions, of its rigorous stoicism. Machiavelli's version is a deliberate use of the old story to show the sordid depth to which men and women have sunk in his own day, his last and most brutal statement about the condition of man in a society that has no one to control it effectively, a dramatic commentary to *The Prince*. Pirandello's version is a criticism of conditions in his time and place, the harsh realities of a closed society. Both are meant to shock us.

Both dramatize a "double" deception. A wealthy old man marries a virtuous young woman who, in exchange for the comforts of life-long "security" is expected to produce an heir. When the woman fails to conceive, the old man in each case agrees to accept a devilish plan that will insure the heir they crave. This common scenario puts religious and moral values to a grueling test.

Both Machiavelli and Pirandello set out to salvage the human situation, each in his own way. Machiavelli indulges in a ruthless and cynical exposure of human nature at its worst, a desperate warning against the depravity of men, the lengths to which people will go to satisfy their lust and greed unless checked by the strong hand of a dedicated ruler.

Pirandello shows how deception serves to set things right, how certain behavior can be excused, under certain inflexible conditions rising from the demands of social and religious pressures. In Machiavelli's play, the deception calls for getting the old man to agree to his wife's taking the mandrake potion and allowing her to sleep with a stranger who will be dragged in for that purpose, since Nicia himself must be spared the "poisonous effects" of the potion: the man who first sleeps with, after she has taken it (he is told) will die from its effects. In Pirandello's play, Uncle Simone agrees to allow the village to think that the child carried by a village girl Tuzza and fathered by Liolà is really his. Self-serving lust is the driving force of Machiavelli's play; greed is the major factor in Pirandello's.

Nicia, the old man in *Mandragola*, has married a young woman, Lucrezia, who cannot produce an heir. Lucrezia's reputed beauty has brought Callimaco back from Paris who, after seeing the young woman decides he must have her. Together with his servant Siro and a hanger-on, Ligurio, to whom Nicia lends money from time to time, Callimaco devises a devilish plan: First he poses as a doctor and gets Ligurio to bring Nicia to him. Spouting Latin phrases made up for the occasion, Callimaco impresses Nicia with his "learning." The good news is that he has a potion that is sure to make Lucrezia conceive. The bad news is that the first man to sleep with her after she has taken the potion will draw all the poison of the mandrake into himself and die. Nicia is about to leave, when Callimaco generously volunteers with the help of his servant Siro and the idler, Ligurio, to roam the streets that night until they find some homeless person to drag back to Lucrezia's bed. The stranger will draw out the "poison" before Nicia sleeps again with his wife. The man is "doomed," but no one will ever find out, Callimaco assures the old man. Nicia agrees.

His wife Lucrezia, on the other hand, will have

no part of this bizarre plot, even when her own mother implores her to go along, reminding her that it's in her best interest to do so: she reminds her daughter that her future, her security is at stake. Does she want to risk everything her marriage has brought her? Again, it is Ligurio who solves the problem: he will have Lucrezia's confessor, Fra Timoteo, talk her into it.

Machiavelli's uncompromising cynicism is embodied in the figure of the monk, who not only turns logic into casuistry in a brilliant argument which includes references to the Old Testament, but also agrees to disguise himself to stand in for Callimaco, who, in rags and with his face screwed up, is the one who will be "found" loitering in the neighborhood and dragged to Lucrezia's bed.

Ligurio first tests the monk with a story about a young girl who, while in the care of nuns, became pregnant by a distant cousin of Nicia's. To avoid scandal, and for a certain price, the monk's help is needed to get the nuns to perform an abortion. The monk agrees; but Ligurio soon returns with the news that the girl has miscarried. The monk, having already agreed to do the unthinkable, is then told the other. "lesser" favor that is needed.

He is waiting and ready for Lucrezia, when her mother brings her to him.

> I have been bent over my books for over two hours, studying this matter; and after careful examination I have found many things that, both in particular and in general, stand in our favor.

Lucrezia's incredulous response is met with an argument that is an inversion of all the moral values Lucrezia has followed all her life.

> As far as the conscience goes, you have to bear in mind this general principle, that, when confronted with a good that is certain and an evil that is uncertain, one must never renounce that good for fear of that evil. Here we have a good that is certain: you will become

pregnant, you will win a soul for our Good Lord; the uncertain evil is that the one who, after the potion, lies with you will die — but it also happens that some do not die. Still, since the thing is doubtful, it is well for Messer Nicia not to run that risk. As for the act itself, to call it a sin is empty talk; for it is the will that sins, not the body. What makes it sinful is to displease the husband, and you please him; to take pleasure in it, and you find only displeasure. Besides, it is the end that must be considered in all things; the end for you is to fill a throne in Heaven, to make your husband happy. The Bible says that the daughters of Lot, believing themselves to be the sole surviving women in the world, mated with their father, and because their intention was good, they did not sin.

Lucrezia caves in. The rest is predictable.

Callimaco is ecstatic the next morning. So are the others. They all have gotten what they wanted without any difficulties. The monk alone expresses some misgiving — not qualms of conscience exactly; rather, a brief worry about the possible consequences of his actions.

There's truth in the old saying that bad company leads men to the gallows; and often a person gets into trouble as much for being too easygoing and good as for being evil. God knows I had no intention of harming anybody: I kept to my cell, I recited my office, I tended my flock; then this devil of a Ligurio crossed my path, who got me to stick a finget in a mess, into which I've sunk my whole arm, and my whole body, and I still don't know where I'll end up. But my one consolation is that when there are many people involved in a thing, many have to look after it.

I have taken time reviewing this extraordinary play to underscore the contrast with Pirandello's *Liolà*,[2] where cynicism — if it can be called that — is of a very different kind.

Liolà, who like Fra Timoteo has the difficult task of convincing a young pious woman that adultery, in her circumstances, is not wrong or immoral or irreligious, seems to have justified his arguments to himself: they ring *true*. He too falls back on religious illustrations, but in this case they are not hypocritical references, inverted truths, but powerful arguments to sustain a righteous and urgent necessity. He is provoked into a defensive action by a providential justice. He does not initiative the seduction, as Callimaco does, nor is lust the motive in his case. He takes action only when he realizes that a sullen and shrewd village girl, Tuzza, is using him to ruin his childhood sweetheart Mita, who, orphaned early in life, living with an aunt and without any prospects, has been forced to marry old Uncle Simone, who expects her to produce an heir in return for lifting her out of her abject poverty. She has failed to do so in her four years of marriage, for which her husband berates her, refusing to entertain the notion that he is impotent, even though his first wife of many years had also failed to produce children. He insults Mita publicly, bemoans not marrying his young second cousin Tuzza instead, and drives Mita, weeping and angry, out of the house. Tuzza, meanwhile, questioned by her mother, reveals that she is pregnant by Liolà. Enraged by Mita's good luck in landing Uncle Simone as a husband and envious of Liolà's affection for Mita, she refuses to marry Liolà (who has made the "honorable" offer) and instead concocts a plan offering her unborn child to Uncle Simone to claim as his own. Since her pregnancy will compromise her reputation anyway (she brazenly tells her mother) she has no qualms in naming Uncle Simone as the father, instead of Liolà. She'll not only gain revenge, she'll have easy access to Uncle Simone's house and a secure future for herself.

There is no one in *Mandragola* who is subjected to humiliation such as Mita's, no one consumed by the jealousy and the desire for revenge displayed by Tuzza, no one forced to protect the innocent as Liolà feels he must. And in that defense there is nothing of the corruption and hypocrisy of Machiavelli's Callimaco. It is Tuzza's trickery that forces him to retaliate. He is furious when he learns of Mita's plight but holds back his anger. He seeks out Mita, who is spending the night alone in her aunt's hut while Aunt Gesa consults a lawyer in town about Mita's predicament, and lays out his plan for her, merciless in his reasoning. She must return to her husband, he tells her. She refuses; they have nothing in common. That's silly, he retorts. "*God* will look after it for me," Mita offers, but Liolà quickly disillusions her.

> God? Oh, sure. . . . He's *supposed* to look after it. He *did* look after it one time — But however good you may be, my pious friend, you can hardly compare yourself with the Virgin Mary!

A heated exchange follows; Mita reminds him that it is not her fault she hasn't conceived. Liolà hammers home the crucial point, that Uncle Simone married her for that one purpose and she has failed him in that respect. It may not be her fault, but someone else will now gain from her failure. The way Tuzza has managed it, Uncle Simone will never believe the child is not his, even if Liolà goes around with a bell around his neck, proclaiming Tuzza's child is *his*! In any case, Mita should be the last person to question what Uncle Simone will say. He, Liolà, has kept silent, denying what Tuzza might have said about him. He has held his tongue for Mita's sake, to make sure that Tuzza does not succeed.

Mita is shocked, but Liola goes on relentlessly: Mita must produce a child in the same way that Tuzza has. Their arguing is interrupted by the coming of Uncle Simone, who wants Mita to go back to the house with him. She is adamant in her refusal, calling out to Aunt Ninfa, next door, to help her get rid of her husband. Ninfa convinces the old man to let Mita stay in her own hut that night, to sleep off her anger and resentment. He finally leaves, going out one door while Liolà surreptitiously slips in through another.

When Mita announces that she is pregnant, Uncle Simone predictably forgets the agreement made with Tuzza. He confesses that he is not the father of Tuzza's child and tries to get Liolà to admit his responsibility and marry the girl, but Liolà is no longer willing to do so, having been rebuffed when Tuzza thought she could do better with Uncle Simone. The play ends with Tuzza trying to stab Liolà while Uncle Simone protects his wife.

Liolà convinces us, as well as Mita, that what he has done is right and proper in the end. We willingly allow the confounding of morality with expediency, of sin and virtue. The end seems to justify the means in this case. In *Liolà* the harsh judgment about human nature is mitigated by the conclusion that a terrible wrong has been made right. The mood of Pirandello's play is one of *reconciliation* rather than despair about man's potential for evil. *Mandragola* has nothing in it to suggest Liolà's magnetic generosity, Mita's helplessness and need for protection, Tuzza's unhappy attempt at deception. There is no hint in it of the moral paradox at the heart of Pirandello's play. In *Mandragola* we find a powerful affirmation of Christian pessimism, a contradiction of the optimistic resolution of moral values found in *Liolà*. Machiavelli's protagonists are painfully aware of their demonic preference for self-indulgence. Pirandello's are fashioned according to the divine image man has concocted in his own soul. Liolà is the epitome of Pirandello's translation of moral "fact" into compelling personal "right"; whereas Machiavelli's monk gives voice to a moral expediency that has nothing to redeem it.

Pirandello's *Liolà* is indeed a romanticized version of Machiavelli's *Mandragola* — which certainly served as the inspiration for it — but there is nothing "romantic" about the harsh conclusion. In spite of the true but unfulfilled love that exists between Mita and Liolà, the action centers on plots and counterplots, deceptions and hypocrisies as unsettling as those Machiavelli depicts, its burden not far removed from that of *Mandragola*: the disgraceful lengths to which people will go — if they can get away with it — to attain their meanest and most selfish ends.

Liolà ultimately defies any comparison. In the impressive gallery of tortured Pirandellian figures, he stands alone. His god-like freedom and his contagious joy produce an aura of innocence and that sense of the miraculous which is the gift of faith. In him, exquisite sensibilities blur and cancel out insidious deception and produce a paradoxical sense of grandeur which raises him above any of the protagonists of the *Mandragola*. Or, from another point of view, he is illusion made flesh, the consummate and marvelous expression of an inspired act of will.

NOTES

1. *Machiavelli's Mandragola*, by Niccolo Machiavelli, trans. Anne and Henry Paolucci, with an Introduction by Henry Paolucci. (originally published by Library of Liberal Arts, New York, 1957; new printing, Bobbs Merrill Company. Indianapolis, 1980; current printing, Paramount).

2. *Naked Masks*, five plays by Luigi Pirandello, translated, with an introduction, by Eric Bentley (E. P. Dutton Co., New York, 1952; rptd Meridian/Penguin Group, etc.).

Monolog Drama: Paul Claudel and Luigi Pirandello

What does Pirandello's theater have in common with Claudel's? Is there any justification for suggesting comparisons between playwrights coming from such different visions and traditions?

On the surface, comparisons seems far-fetched between "the father of the contemporary theater" (as Robert Brustein refers to Pirandello) and the French playwright, whose religious vision is the base of large spectacular productions (like those of Percy MacKaye at the turn of the century, here in America). Claudel's Catholic dramas would seem far removed from Pirandello's *avant la lettre* existential theater. In fact, many critics would remind us that Claudel is no longer a vital force in today's theater, that he remains interesting only to a few scattered academics, whereas Pirandello's is still felt in today's theater and will continue to be felt for many years to come.

One discerning critic has pointed out that the modern theater has in fact "caught up" with Claudel. Writing of the first version of *Tete d'or* (1889), Henri Peyre asserts emphatically that "no play could have been further removed from the theater then in fashion than the dishevelled lyricism of that play"; yet,

> the very same dramas which failed to start a ripple over the literary waters of the last decade of the nineteenth century and which not one academic critic deigned to notice are those which, sixty years after or more, are enjoyed when performed for informed audiences. They are the theme of exhaustive studies by critics; they arouse enthusiasm even among the iconoclast young. . .
> . *Tete d'or*, which Claudel never allowed to be staged as

Read at a Paul Claudel Society meeting in Texas, 1976. (Revised) long as he was alive, although he had declared it to be the first significant step in his career as dramatist, has lost little of its disconcerting weirdness after six decades; indeed it might seem to be marked with all the mannerisms of a period piece in the Symbolist (and exacerbated romantic) mood. Yet it was lauded as "marvelous," dramatically moving and richly enigmatic when performed in 1959 at the Theatre de France with the blessing of De Gaulle and his Minister of Culture, Malraux. . . . [O]ne of the most learned students of Claudel today, Professor Jacques Petit, devoted a volume to it, to be followed by another scholarly study in 1971 . . . by Aimé Becker.[1]

Even though he appears on the surface to be diametrically opposed to Pirandello's handling of the stage, Claudel was moving in a similar direction with insights no less innovative and with a sense of theater no less discerning than Pirandello's. He seems to favor an expanding stage and rich settings very different from Pirandello's; but like the Italian playwright, he became fascinated, according to Jacques Petit and Jean-Pierre Kempf, in *Claudel on the Theatre*, "by all facets of directing, setting, acting, costuming, and the technical aspects of dramatic production." In all his concerns with the techniques of dramatic performance, as well as in all that he had to say about dramatic art, Claudel's overriding concern, Petit and Kempf tell us, and as Claudel himself acknowledged, was to "restore the theatre to its original purity," continuing in that respect the "tradition of Copeau."[2] His intention, is very like that of Pirandello,[3] who had made clear in his own way that he meant to give theater a new direction.

Petit and Kempf agree that Claudel "has nothing that could be called a dramatic system — nothing to be pieced together mosaic-fashion to make up a "treatise on dramatic art"; but they assure us that "the few basic demands" Claudel makes on the theater show a more or less consistent development as his interest (always essentially poetic) ranged over every aspect of the art, spilling over into ballet and mime, opera, and the semi-dramatic spectacles of non-European cultures. They point out that for Claudel "'creation' does not stop with publication of a work, and that production does not merely interpret a play but [as he wrote to Pottechev as early as 1897] completes it, gives it an outward form." In his effort to articulate total theater, he

> calls upon the services not only of the scenic designer, the producer, and the actor, but also on those of the dancer, the composer, and the film maker. Words are not enough; at certain moments they need the support of music, and then the music turns to singing and calls for movement, and movement becomes dancing; and then sometimes the very presence of the actors is too immediate, and only film can give the play what it needs. . . .[4]

Experiments of this kind surely validate the current interest shown in the work of Brecht. In our context — recalling the words of Henri Peyre — they certainly validate our own contemporary interest in Claudel.

Howsoever one reacts to Claudel's range of sets — from simple realistic ones to extravagant displays — the playwright's intentions are sound and very modern: "The scene," he tells us, "should be . . . not a mere background for the actors, but a projection of the text itself, stressing and clarifying the poet's meaning." In some plays he uses (like O'Neill often does) a symbolic letter, like the *omega* of a chair, or of a swing or hammock. But he just as often insists on absolute realism. "A door is meant to open and close."[5] In this sense, he is very much like Pirandello, who often sticks to the literal realism of the stage as the basic term in an equation meant to undermine external phenomena and restructure reality from within.

Claudel regarded diction and gestures on stage as all important. Both had to be subordinated to the text, of course, but handled properly they could be significant in articulating meaning. At Helleran, near Dresden, where a German adaptation of *L'Annonce faite à marie* was staged by the "experimental theatre" of the Institute of Art, he was struck by the "sculptural beauty of which gesture was capable." But it was Nijinky, who gave him "an even better insight into the powers of expression of the body." "He takes our most misused gestures, as Virgil took our words and images, and transports them into the blissful realm of all that is intelligent, powerful, and ethereal." Petit and Kempf underscore this comment, pointing out that what Claudel is describing is the world of "art and of poetry, of which Virgil is for him the most perfect expression." The movement from poetry to music is a natural one. "The ideal . . . would be for music to spring from poetry, as poetry springs from prose, and prose from silence and the formless mutterings of the mind." Music can extend and complete poetry; it "can play the part of the chorus, express the feelings of the audience, and reply to the action. In fact, music 'listens'."[6]

Claudel charged his friend Darius Milhaud with the task of showing how music necessarily comes out of words as they become truly poetic. Milhaud was quick to see how the use of Shadow Actors could produce effects comparable to music accompaniments. In some cases, actors were indeed to have doubles following them, as if trailing shadows. Petit and Kempf explain: "As the second actor did not speak, the intention seemed to be to dissociate speech and gesture to some extent, and to give the latter its full breadth and meaning through the 'double'. The resulting slowness recalled the rhythm of No drama."[7]

Pirandello's use of two sets of actors in *Six Characters in Search of an Audience* and *Each in His Own Way* provides an intriguing parallel. Although his intention is different, the idea of using "doubles" to articulate the art of acting is essentially the same as Claudel's. In both cases, such a vision suggested the "inner stage" or what Claudel calls *Guignol*. For Claudel, the normal stage would be occupied by a chorus, "as an intermediary between the actors and the audience." In some plays, an Announcer was cast in the role of the chorus. The actors then became "voiced" puppets, at a distance, even in a dream, a "guided dream."[8] For Pirandello, the stage was a multi-level of psychological awareness. The "theater plays" are the obvious example of how a realistic stage, usually a Sicilian setting, sets into motion an "inner stage" resulting in a constant oscillating between the two.

Although they seem to have gone in different directions, all that has been said so far about Claudel's unusual approach to theatre suggests Pirandello's vision of the expanded stage. Both also saw the role of the actor in a new light. Claudel "emphasized frequently . . . the 'non-existence' of his characters, which were simply divergent and contradictory aspects of himself." In one context, he "expressed a very similar idea with a different justification — that his characters were simply the actors in a 'parable'." Pirandello's "myth" plays at once come to mind. *The Mountain Giants* can indeed be regarded as a parable about art and its limits, the struggle for definition and communication, what Claudel describes as the poet speaking *for* the people, not *for their benefit but on their behalf*. For Claudel (and ultimately for Pirandello as well) the poet is a solitary figure, "the only one with a face of his own speaking amid a semicircle of voices, which, simply by being there, lure and compel him to speech."[9] This statement could just as easily describe Pirandello's six characters, whose voices lured and compelled him to abandon all else and provide the drama for which they exist.

Like Pirandello, Claudel sees drama as the movement from life to "parable" and acting as emotional communication through symbols. It was an old dream of his to make the transition from daily life to drama or parable obvious in the acting, a dream which gave rise to his ideal of "the 'theatre in process of birth'." The third version of *Tête d'or* would have shown prisoners of war in a German camp rehearsing the play, bringing it to life and gradually living it themselves, up to the point — quite easy to imagine — when it is impossible to tell where the play ends and life begins. . . . *Tête d'or* shows that this is neither a trick nor a superficial demonstration of theatrical illusion. Apart from the meaning it gives the action, we can see in it an appeal to the audience to become, not merely spectators, but accomplices and even participants. The drama is, after all, their own.[10]

Rehearsals as part of a script are the perfect means for bringing the audience into the experience: the "reality" of the stage is a work-in-progress, the actors in and out of their assumed roles are like the spectators. The distance between the stage and "real life" disappears in plays like the third version Claudel contemplated for *Tête d'or* or Pirandello's *Tonight We Improvise*.

What has been described so far about Claudel's theater and Pirandello's may best be defined as "monolog" art. For both, the playwright is indeed the only face, the only voice; actors are simply extensions of the playwright's struggle for definition and artistic identity. It is not inconceivable that Pirandello, whose early success was due to French productions staged by French directors, should come under the influence of Claudel, to some extent. By the same token, it is almost certain that Pirandello's success in France did much to assure Claudel's later theatrical revival.

Whatever the case, Claudel's insistence on the importance of "Shadow Actors" as the playwright's many-timbred voice and Pirandello's layering of roles suggest similar dramatic concerns. In his efforts to return to the very origins of drama, in his attempt to restore to dramatic art its pristine purity, Claudel may have found other expressions and may have been drawn to other ways of making his point; but the essential idea is not far removed from that of Pirandello, whose commitment was to restructure the modern stage as the vehicle for his new vision of dramatic art. Both were in fact attempting to translate the "third voice of poetry" (as T. S. Eliot calls the art of drama) into the first voice, the lyric voice, the poet "talking to himself or nobody."[11]

Claudel saw the actor, and therefore the character, as a "gesture and a voice" and insisted that the audience must join him in making it so. "All these various beings have given up their own preoccupations and personalities. They have handed over the right of speech to the poet. All that remains is attentive silence and a strange state of collective, almost hypnotic, receptivity."[12] The drama that emerges is of course very different from Pirandello's. Claudel, after all, openly acknowledges and puts forward in his plays his Catholic faith; for Pirandello, religion is translated into belief in the self, a compassion for one's fellow man, a humanitarian concern. Claudel's drama is a poetic assertion of the divine; Pirandello's is a compelling claim for man's integral goodness. Claudel's world is a vision of the divine illuminating this earthly existence, Pirandello's is indeed a "vale of tears" but without divine intervention.

Pirandello describes his settings in "almost maniacal" fullness and the events depicted are drawn from the hard, often cruel spectacle of human beings struggling against great odds, trying desperately to extricate themselves from an unyielding and impassive destiny. In such settings, the humble village dwelling or the middle-class bourgeois home is just that (*Liolà, The License, The Jar, Right You Are!]If You Think So], Each in His Own Way, Lazarus,* etc.), but it also serves as a "crazy mirror" reflecting the limitations of the stage, the paradoxical "reality" of the inner stage in the "theater plays." His characters, accordingly, become — in Claudel's language —"silhouettes." By means of dramatic confrontations that involve the audience at every moment (again, especially in the "theater plays"), these "silhouettes" force a new dramatic *space* to emerge. Writing about *Six Characters,* Francis Fergusson has perhaps expressed it best:

The action of the play is "to take the stage" — with all that this suggestive phrase implies. The real actors and the director want to take it for the realistic purposes — vain or (with the box office in mind) venal — of their rehearsal. Each of the characters wants to take it for the rationalized myth which is, or would be, his very being. Pirandello sees human life itself as theatrical: as aiming at, and only to be realized in, the tragic epiphany. He inverts the convention of modern realism; instead of pretending that the stage is not the stage at all, but the familiar parlor, he pretends that the familiar parlor is not real, but a stage, containing many "realities."[13]

Pirandello's characters are not meant to adapt to the traditionally realistic sets or to the objective realistic world they represent, the pre-ordained conventional settings in which their creator initially places them. In *Six Characters* the "real" actors and their director observe that the insistence of the intruders on reworking things is no way to make theater. In *Right You Are!* Laudisi tells us in his emphatic and almost convincing skepticism that to look for external confirmation of things is no way to interpret life. In *Henry IV*, the madman's insistence on his make-believe world tells us that we are all rewriting our lives, according to some internal principle — consciously or unconsciously. The conclusion of all this is not always clear or even apparent to us, but we are very much aware that it is larger than what is before us and greater than the limits of the setting and what is there spoken. Through these levels of awareness as they are defined on the stage, we come to recognize the dichotomy between familiar conventions and inner conviction; the formal actors, of *Six Characters*, Laudisi, Henry in his isolation help to articulate and make explicit that dichotomy which is the drama of the *expanding* stage.

In Claudel it is more a physical phenomena than a psychological one; and his characters reflect the religious base of his vision. Yet there is a common denominator in Claudel's saints and sinners and

Pirandello's *esclusi* or outcasts. Pirandello's characters often find their solution to the problem of identity in a retreat into what seems to the rest of the world (and the audience) a kind of obsession, a form of madness. Claudel's find their salvation in holding firm to another kind of absolute. In both, the characters must "go it alone," must find their true configuration on their own, very often at the expense of the solid life around them. And so, even though widely separated in their subject matter, Claudel and Pirandello come together in characters who find their bearings in the single voice of the poet-dramatist — in Claudel's assertion of the power of faith in God; in Pirandello's assertion of the power of faith in man, a certainty that takes us to the very threshold of non-art, of fragmented experience held together by what is suggested rather than what is said and done — the threshold of the contemporary theater of the Absurd.[14]

Pirandello's "mad" emperor, Henry IV, disorients his visitors and avenges himself on them through long explanations and revelations; The Father in *Six Characters* (as well as Step-Daughter and The Mother) tries desperately to make his compelling life-drama meaningful as stage-drama, forcing us to consider, at every moment, the oscillation between one and the other, the life-drama which is also stage business and the stage business which is trying to reach out into the wider life-drama; Ilse and Cotrone in *The Mountain Giants* struggle to convince each other of their respective notions about the purpose and nature of dramatic art and in the end are forced to test their convictions against an unresponsive world. *Tonight We Improvise* — like Claudel's "dream" for *Tête d'or*, a rehearsal in a German prison camp — is a reaching out not so much for social consciousness in the usual sense but for an awareness of the responsibilities each of us must assume, responsibilities which are total and dramatic expression of the fact that we are all saints and sinners, all victims and oppressors, and that compassion — which is also Christian charity — is the *sine qua non* of the drama of life. Mario Baratto reminds us that nothing is really improvised and nothing is really resolved in this play. We carry away not a content but a form of revelation, the monolog voice of the poet-dramatist which resonates in all of us, the need to build the very road on which we walk, every day of our lives, of the urgent necessity for demolishing the idols and icons we are given to live by and for restoring the Socratic mystery that is the voice of faith and the beginning of true knowledge.

> Ce tháâtre concu comme un tribunal est un nouvel acte de confiance du dramaturge, un refus torturé du mystère et du silence. Pirandello s'arrête ici: au seiul d'un tháâtre qui serait situá a nouveau dans un contexte historique et social plu prácis, qui commencerait à préciser, loin des équivoques, les responsabilités de chacun: qui nous permettait de distinguer les bourreaux des victimes, les oppresseurs des opprimés.[15]

The playwright who restructured the stage for the monolog drama of Christian faith is, in final analysis, not much removed from the playwright who restructured the stage for the monolog drama of Socratic questioning. In one of his last statements on the theater, Claudel explains that "human drama is not complete until a superhuman element comes into it." That element can be good or evil (the gods in the *Iliad*, the witches in *Macbeth*, Phaedra). "But," he goes on emphatically, isolating for the moment Racine's *Phèdre*:

> What gives the drama its poignancy — because it is not only Phaedra's, but Racine's too — is the question it asks of the conscience of anyone who is inspired, who is both victim and accomplice of an unknown, ambivalent, and questionable power. At the very beginning of tragedy, on the very threshold of that terrible door from which so many masterpieces were to emerge, old Aeschylus set up the imposing figure of the Trojan prophetess, accusing her seducer Apollo:

Apollo! Apollo! God of the Gate, my Death-dealer! For thou has destroyed me utterly, this second time! . . . Why then do I wear these mockeries of myself, this scepter, and these prophetic chaplets around my neck? I will destroy you before I meet my fate! Go, accursed that you are! God and enrich with doom another instead of me.

How often I have thought of those terrifying lines. . . . It is the same with Phaedra. In vain she looks to an embrace as something human which may heal the ancient wound. Nothing can help her. In the last lines of the tragedy she turns toward us a face petrified with the same horror as made the face of Cassandra glow pale . . . the face of the Gorgon reflected in the shield of Perseus. This is the *denouement* of *Phèdre*. You know those incredible lines, which I cannot read without a shudder, in which, from the depths of Hell, she flings forth a despairing cry to that Father in Heaven from whom she has her being. It was right and natural that after writing them the pen should break of its own accord in the mighty hand that held it.[16]

Claudel wrote those words in 1954, when Pirandello had already been dead for eighteen years; but in their profound insight into the madness that lurks inside us all, in their compassionate awareness of the paradox of evil, they might indeed have been written by Pirandello. For, like the Italian playwright, Claudel understood the strength of human frailty; and in his own despairing cry to that Father in Heaven from whom we derive being and to whom we hurl our invectives, Claudel displays the profound Pirandellian conviction that we must all settle accounts in our own way, in our own image. In him we sense that same large sympathy for human error, the same awareness and suspicion of ready-made formulas, the same firm belief in Socratic obstinacy in the service of truth.

From another direction, Pirandello reminds us that God is indeed in all of us and that it is up to us to find our own measure of divinity. His monolog drama, like Claudel's, leads us to what ultimately will enable us to restructure not only the stage in our image but also to refashion that very image of the self according to a new awareness of a consistent and universal truth.

NOTES

1. Henri Peyre, "Claudel: Bibliographical Spectrum," *Review of National Literatures*, Vol. IV, Number 2. Series Editor, Anne Paolucci (Council on National Literatures [Griffon House Publications], New York, 1973), p. 97.

2. Jacques Petit and Jean-Marie Kempf, *Claudel on the Theatre*, translated by Christine Trollope (University of Miami Press, Coral Gables, 1972), book jacket; cf. "Preface," *passim*. Generalizing on the conclusions drawn by Petit and Kempf, Peyre writes: "If ever Claudel's literary and artistic statements are collected in one volume (some of them have been compiled in a book [*Claudel on the Theatre*], readers will be entertained by the successive — at times nearly simultaneous — pros and cons, anathemas and eulogies uttered by that typical Frenchman, in tones equally peremptory and self-assured. Our paltry critics' minds might be reassured if we could trace a clear evolution from one point of view to another, from romantic and rhetorical exaltation, for instance, to classical restraint, or from the pale and disembodied muses of the Symbolist poets to the baroque sumptuousness of *Le Souliere de satin*. But no such curve can, in all fairness, be suggested, Claudel confessed repeatedly to being a hot-tempered man, whose wrath had to boil over and spill invectives (especially to those who appeared to him as enemies of his faith). The purgation once effected, he recovered his balance; he could then become, if not a model of charity, at least indifferent and almost lenient." (Claudel and the French Literary Tradition," *Review of National Literatures*, p. 23.)

3. For detailed analyses of the plays of Pirandello, see Anne Paolucci: *Pirandello's Theater: The Recovery of the Modern Stage for Dramatic Art* (Southern Illinois University Press, Carbondale, 1974; rptd Gtiffon House Publications, Smyrna DE, 2002).

4. *Claudel on the Theatre*, pp. xii-xiv.

5. *Ibid.*, p. xv.

6. *Ibid.*, pp. xvi-xvii; 17.

7. *Ibid.*, p. xviii.

8. *Ibid.*, p. xviii-xix.

9. *Ibid.*, p. xx.

10. *Ibid.*, p. xxi.

11. T. S. Eliot, "The Three Voices of Poetry," *On Poets and Poetry* (Noonday Press, New York, 1943, etc.), pp. 96, 112.

12. See, Mario Baratto, "Le Théatre de Pirandello," in Jacques Jacquot, ed., *Réalisme et Poésie au Théatre* (Paris, 1960), p. 183.

13. Francis Fergusson, *The Idea of a Theater* (Princeton, 1949), pp. 187-188. Cf. Marion Peter Holt's discussion of this aspect of Pirandello's treatment of the stage in José López Rubio (Twayne, Boston, 1980).

14. For an interesting account of the "logic" of the descent from monolog "expressionism" through the "Absurd" into aesthetic "silence," see Victor Lange, "Expressionism: A Topological Essay," *Review of National Literatures*, Series Editor, Anne Paolucci, Vol 9 (1978), *German Expressionism*, pp. 26-46; and, more particularly, his "Language as the Topic of Modern Fiction," in P. F. Ganz, ed., *The Discontinuous Tradition* (Oxford, 1971), p. 260ff.

15. Baratto, p. 194.

16. *Claudel on the Theater*, p. 187.

"Improvisation" as "Script":
Carlo Goldoni and Luigi Pirandello

Pirandello regarded Goldoni as the pivotal figure in the history of the modern Italian Theater, the master dramatist who restored the traditional script to theater, undermining the popular commercial or professional actors' theater, the *commedia dell'arte*.[1] The major actors of the *commedia* had achieved "stardom" for having mastered and identified with a particular character or role; the really great ones had perfected all the possibilities of a certain type-casting, using that knowledge on stage to great advantage. The result was noteworthy, but unrepeatable in that no complete script, as such, existed in most cases, only outlines of the various roles for the major stereotypes..

Goldoni's purpose was to "unmask" the actors of the *commedia*, who over the years had provided what audiences liked to see and for which they were willing to pay. These constituted, in fact, a kind of "trade guild," became "writers" themselves, providing the outlines for the "living," seemingly improvised theater the public enjoyed, using material best suited for their acting abilities.

In his brilliant *Mémoires pour servir à l'histoire de sa vie et à celle de son théâtre*,[2] Goldoni tells us how it happened that he began to write "scripts" for *commedia dell'arte* actors, and how that led him to the idea of "reforming the masks of Italian comedy and of substituting comedies for farces." Cesare D'Abres, the celebrated *Pantalone* of Gerolamo Medebach's internationally famous theater company had sought

---

Read at a special weekend program featuring Goldoni's Servant of Two Masters *at the American Repertory Theatre, Cambridge Massachusetts (Robert Brustein, Artistic Director), and published in* American Repertory Theatre News, *Vol. XII, No. 3, May 1992. (Revised and expanded.)*

out Goldoni, introducing himself unabashedly as an "an actor . . . in need of an author." After many thrusts and counter-thrusts, Goldoni agreed to the request but, as he hastens to explain, his purpose from the beginning was to get D'Abres to appear on stage "à visage découvert," without his masks; that, he writes unambiguously, "was my project, that was my chief aim."

Goldoni's extended account of the experience makes for a little play in itself. It must certainly have excited Pirandello when he first read it. Allardyce Nicoll, in his splendidly illustrated *The World of Harlequin*,[3] cites the passage at length and then notes that what came out of the experience for Goldoni was, first of all, the play *Tonin Bella Grazia* (1745), which led "through the first version of *Il servitore di due padroni* (1746) . . . on to *La vedova scaltra* (1748) and the later glories of the Goldoni canon."

In the same passage about D'Abres, Goldoni states very clearly why he was convinced that the theatrical masks had to go. They had no doubt been useful for "characterization" in the large open theaters of the ancient Greeks and Romans. But the theaters of his day, he noted, were enclosed and small. He also observed, looking more deeply into the matter, that with respect to ancient drama "the emotions and sentiments had not then been brought to such delicacy as is demanded today, we now want the actor to have a soul, and a soul under a mask is like fire under ashes."

Students of Hegel's theory of drama will surely recognize in that observation the very basis for the 19th-century German philosopher's broad distinction between ancient and modern comedy as well as tragedy. And students of Shakespeare criticism will recall that, under Hegel's influence, A. C. Bradley applied that insight not only in his Oxford lectures on the great Shakespearean tragedies[4] but also in his brilliant essay "The Rejection of Falstaff."[5] In the latter, Bradley explains that the source of our "sympathetic delight" in Falstaff is his "humorous superiority to everything serious and the freedom of soul enjoyed in it." Hegel had insisted that the same can be said also of Shakespeare's most vulgar comic characters, like Stephano, Trinculo, and Pistol, for example, who, while remaining "sunk in their vulgarity" are yet shown to be "fit for anything," to have an entirely "free existence and to be, in short, what great men are."[6]

Pirandello may have read some Hegel while studying for his degree in linguistics at the University of Bonn, but one need not spend time confirming or dismissing the possibility: what we can say for certain is that he appreciated the important role of comedy generally, and especially Goldoni's role in revitalizing Italian comedy.

Pirandello emphasizes Goldoni's contribution as a turning point in the history of the Italian theater, to be sought not in the subordinate characters as such (Shakespeare and others had already introduced such characters) but in raising those ordinary, bourgeois, simple characters to prominence, giving them comedies of their own. "The little housemaid, for example, suddenly becomes, like Mirandolina, the center of a comedy of her own; and many others come forward, *en masse*, to stand there and bicker freely in the streets of Chioggia." Truffaldino is another such character.[7]

The gullible, miserly masters, the double set of lovers, the former stock characters, the intrigues of mistaken identities, etc. are all present in *Servant of Two Masters*, as part of the *commedia* legacy; but it is Truffaldino who takes over the play, almost larger than life, and becomes the center of the comedy. His ingenuity, like Falstaff's, has no limits and sets him apart. He is indeed a match even for the great Shakespearean *truffatore*. His great scene, setting out dinners for each of his "masters" (while making preparations for his own lavish meal), ends up being what one critic, describing a New York production, called "an orgy among the edibles . . . giving the stage the general appearance of a delicatessen store wrecked by a tornado."

Commedia dell'arte, in Goldoni's "rehandling," provided the stage energy for a new European theater. Instead of shrinking into tired mediocrity, the *commedia*, revitalized and restructured by Goldoni's genius, inspired later playwrights, who derived stimulation and excitement from it. Pirandello points out that Goldoni's rival, Carlo Gozzi, had tried in his own way to save the *commedia*; but it was the author of *Servant of Two Masters* who realized perspicaciously that the possibilities for the future lay *not* in salvaging the *commedia* but in creating a new theater that would make the fullest use of its enduring strengths while allowing new forces to redirect it.

Pirandello gives Goldoni full credit for having put the Italian theater back on track, but the idea of improvisation and the attraction of the *commedia dell'arte* was not lost on him. In *Tonight We Improvise* (the third of his so-called "theater plays"), we have a striking dramatic commentary on improvisation by actors who are well into their parts and, as in the *commedia dell'arte*, have been given only outlines of the scenes thay are to play. He certainly must have had the *commedia dell'arte* in mind when he has the actors challenge the director and drive him off stage at the end of the play and announce to the audience: "We don't need him! All we need is a script!" Like Goldoni before him, Pirandello is repudiating the idea of improvisation but — in his case — in a striking format paradoxically much like that of *commedia dell'arte*.

Worth mentioning, in passing at least, is that Pirandello, like Goldoni before him — who wrote many of his plays in his native "Venetian" — chose to write his early plays in his native language: in his case, the "dialect" of Agrigento. Although in both cases, the plays are almost impossible to read, Pirandello's "dialect" plays strangely enough come through when actually heard on stage. Possibly, Goldoni's too can be grasped when actually seen and heard (although I cannot be sure, in this case, not having seen a Goldoni play performed in the Venetian "dialect").

In the larger perspective: Pirandello must be credited for the restructured theater of his own day, in which he retained realism or naturalism, redefining it in new ways, just as Goldoni had preserved and enhanced the best features of the *commedia dell'arte* in his plays.

Later drama expanded the possibilities of the idiosyncratic character — the legacy of *commedia dell'arte* — first in the realistic plays of Ibsen, then the psychological and painful excursions of Strindberg's drama and O'Neill's, later in the political, social, and regional drama of Arthur Miller, Tennessee Williams and others. The innovative theater of Pirandello himself, of Beckett, Ionesco, Pinter, Albee, Anhouilh, Giraudoux and others has forced us still deeper into the probing of personality, as we seek objective correlatives for the fragmented *persona* struggling to find its identity in the shards of mirrored self-consciousness.

We will never again be able to accept, as the Greeks did, *action* as the most important single element of drama. In the modern theater, action has become a function of character and revolves around it. The idiosyncratic personality of modern drama harbors good and evil, is in many ways unpredictable — the kind of dramatic figure that first asserted itself in the restructured types of the *commedia dell'arte*, refashioned by Shakespeare and his contemporaries, as well as Molière and others after him. It has come fully into its own in the modern world where, as Hegel reminds us, the Christian dispensation has made individual redemption and therefore individual freedom possible.

It was Goldoni who first gave voice and presence to that democratic spirit, depicting the most ordinary men and women in their full dramatic potency. And it was Pirandello, "father of the contemporary theater,"[8] who set drama on a new course once again, who recognized the new existential imperative for subjective correlatives that would translate the deepest human emotions, the unending search for personal identity in valid terms for the contemporary stage.

NOTES

1. See, "Pirandello's Introduction to the Italian Theater," translated by Anne Paolucci, in *Genius of the Italian Theater*, ed. Eric Bentley (Mentor Books/New American Library, New York, 1964), pp. 11-29.

2. Paris, 1788.

3. Cambridge: 1963, 1976.

4. *Shakespearean Tragedy* (Macmillan and Company, London, 1950).

5. *Oxford Lectures on Poetry* (Macmillan and Company, London, 1950).

6. See the sections on comedy in Anne and Henry Paolucci, eds., *Hegel on Tragedy* (Doubleday Co, New York, 1962; Harper & Row, New York 1974; Greenwood Press, 1978; new printing Griffon House Publications, Smyrna DE, 2001).

7. "Introduction to the Italian Theater," *op cit.*

8. See Robert Brustein's comments about Pirandello in Anne Paolucci, *Pirandello's Theater: The Recovery of the Modern Stage for Dramatic Art* (Southern Illinois University Press, Carbondale, 1974; rptd Griffon House Publications, Smyrna, DE, 2002), especially pp. 5-6.

PART FOUR
THE LARGER VIEW

The Literary Societies of New York: Call Them Eccentric.
Call Them Escapist. Call Them the Salons of 90's.

THE NEW YORK TIMES, SUNDAY, MARCH 27, 1994

'Riverrun' to Cyberspace:

Answers to the Quiz

Wherein Also Lies a Reader's Guide to the City's Literary Societies

Here are the answers to the quiz on pages 1 and 9, along with the names and available information about local societies devoted to each.

1. SIR ARTHUR CONAN DOYLE
There are three local branches of the Baker Street Irregulars:
The Priory Scholars, c/o William Nadel, 235 West 71st Street, New York, N.Y., 10023.
The Montague Street Lodgers, c/o Thomas Utecht, 1676 East 55th Street, Brooklyn, N.Y., 11234.
Watson's Tin Dispatchers, c/o Richard Kitts, 35 Van Cortland Avenue, Staten Island, N.Y., 10301.

2. HENRIK IBSEN
Ibsen Society of America, DeKalb Hall III, Pratt Institute, Brooklyn, N.Y., 11205. $15 a year; 130 members. (718) 636-3790.

3. LUIGI PIRANDELLO
Pirandello Society of America, c/o Anne Paolucci, St. John's University, Jamaica, Queens, 11439.

4. MAUD HART LOVELACE
Betsy-Tacy Society, c/o Andrea Shaw, 224 East 11th Street, Apt. 20, New York, N.Y. 10003.

5. ANTHONY TROLLOPE
Trollope Society of America. $40 a year; 350 members. (212) 758-1355.

6. JANE AUSTEN
Jane Austen Society of North America-New York, $15 a year; 450 members. C/o Barbara Heilering, 408 West 57th Street, New York, N.Y. 10019.

7. JAMES JOYCE
James Joyce Society. $7.50 a year;

A recent issue of the journal issued by the Betsy-Tacy Society.

250 members. Call Phil Lyman, (212) 719-4448.
"Finnegans Wake" Reading Group. $1 a meeting. (212) 719-4448 or (516) 764-3119.

8. REX STOUT'S NERO WOLFE BOOKS
The Wolfepack, $25 a year; 350 members. P.O. Box 822, Ansonia Station. New York, N.Y. 10023.

OTHER SOCIETIES
There are many other societies with literary themes, some devoted to a single writer and some not. Here is an eclectic selection:
The Mark Twain Society. 200 members. (212) 255-9640.

The New York C. S. Lewis Society, $10 a year, 550 members. C/o Clara Sarrocco, 84-23 77th Avenue, Glendale, Queens, 11385.
The W. B. Yeats Society of New York, $10 a year, $7 for students; 200 members. C/o the National Arts Club, 15 Gramercy Park South, New York, N.Y. 10003.
The Books Conference (part of the East Coast Hangout, a Greenwich Village-based computer network). (212) 255-3839. Cost: $19.95-$49.95 per month. Some discounts available.
The Literary Society, 270 Convent Avenue, Suite 10-B, New York, N.Y. 10031. Concentrates on works by African-American authors. 75 members.
The Philolexian Society, (212) 853-3728. Meets at Columbia College, features "bad poetry" contest and debates. Open to the public.
The Grolier Club, (212) 838-6690. Martin Antonetti, librarian. A nonprofit organization with membership roll, with exhibitions open to the public.
The Brooke Astor Reading Group. By invitation (from Mrs. Astor) only. 20 members.
The Conservators Club, offered through the New York Public Library for contributors of $1,250 to $5,000. Features discussions of books with their authors, sometimes prior to publication.
Sisters in Crime group for people interested in women and mysteries. There are meetings every other month at the Cornelia Street Cafe, and people should call the cafe at (212) 989-0319 for details. C. L. H.

Literary Salons of the 90's

the **PIRANDELLO society of america** INC. _____

FOUNDED IN 1958

General correspondence, submissions (with diskette [if possible], double-spaced 15-20 pp. typescript, and SASE), and membership dues ($15 ind., $30 lib. [add $5. for foreign membership]) should be addressed to Dr. Anne Paolucci, Eng. Dept., St. John's University, 8000 Utopia Pkwy, Jamaica, NY 11439.

TOWARD A NATIONAL THEATER

In an interview with TV host Dick Cavett some years ago, Italian superstar Marcello Mastroianni — appearing with famed director Federico Fellini — reminded us of the continuing difference between the theater environment in Italy and that in England, France, Spain, the United States or even Russia and Germany. All those other countries, he said, have a national theater audience: Italy has not. Even Rome, he pointed out, has only a *regional* theater audience. The same is true of Milan, Florence, Naples, Turin, Bologna, Palermo, Genoa, etc. He recalled his "big theatrical success" of some years earlier, when he played Rudolph Valentino in a kind of musical — a success measured by a run of only six months. But six months in Rome — he quickly explained — is like a four-year run in London, Paris, or New York. A successful run in "small-town" Rome is usually about two months. Six months was phenomenal.

He made clear that unlike the audiences in Paris, London, or New York, audiences in Italian cities are restricted culturally to their home ground. Although Italy and Germany and the United States became nations at approximately the same time, the unification of Germany and the United States proved much more enduring, culturally. Germany and the United States in the late 19th century joined England, France, and Spain with more or less unified national identities and with national cultural capitals. Berlin and New York became national cultural centers like Paris and London. The expectation in the 1860s was that Florence (not Rome, oddly enough) would be the Italian equivalent.

Historians of drama and aesthetics tell us that a

First appeared in Canadian Journal of Italian Studies. *(Revised.)*

full flowering of art is possible only with a mature national-cultural self-consciousness, concentrated in a national capital. Dramatists can start anywhere in the provinces, in the mid-West, in regional theaters; but if they are to perfect the "third voice of poetry"[1] and transform their particularized possibilities into genuine artistic universality, there must be a national cultural capital with a national theater to which they can aspire.

The pull of Rome was felt by many of Italy's provinces, following unification. There was much talk that Italy would soon have a genuine national literary language, even though in the decade of 1860-1870 only a minority could understand and speak the so-called national language — the language of Dante, Petrarch, Boccaccio, Ariosto, and Machiavelli — much less write it. The new national language would be — some said — the language of Tuscany spoken with a Roman accent, despite Dante's notorious contempt for that variety of Italian, as spoken in his day. We know how much self-conscious attention Italian writers have given to the question of an Italian literary language since the days of Dante. We know what Machiavelli said about it, what efforts were made by academics to standardize an Italian literary language through the centuries, we know how hard regional dramatists like Goldoni (and Pirandello himself, later) worked to translate their regional vitality into their artificially-acquired mastery of the emergent national language. We know of Manzoni's tremendous effort to secure natural living roots for that new artificially-acquired language by sharpening his ear in Tuscany.

In preparing with my husband a long article on "Dante and the 'Quest for Eloquence' in India's Vernacular Languages,"[2] I was impressed — through unexpected, unchartered parallels in this case — with the peculiar development of culture and language in Italy. In that article, we traced similarities between what happened in Italy, linguistically, from Dante's time to the days of Tagore, the well-known Nobel-prize laureate who wrote in Bengali even while Ghandi was taking up the struggle to make Hindi (or, as he preferred to call it, Hindustani) the national language of India. The 13th and 20th centuries suddenly became a fascinating superimposition, reinforcing what I already knew and providing me with a fresh conviction about the interaction of cultural and political forces.

In helping to write that essay, I often thought of Pirandello's interest in languages, his efforts to universalize his Sicilian or, more precisely, the dialect of Agrigento, by making it speak the national language of Italy— an interest that grew in part at least out of his studies in linguistics at the University of Bonn, where he wrote his dissertation on "The Sounds and Phonetic Development of the Dialect of Girgenti."

His early plays were written in the "dialect" of Agrigento and only later "translated" by the playwright himself into "formal" Italian. He illustrates most impressively what T. S. Eliot singled out as the crucial combination that makes for greatness in a new author: "strong local flavor and unintentional universality."[3] Pirandello showed that it could be done, that a writer could raise himself from a particular, regional, or provincial inspiration to a genuinely national and therefore universal literary art. As it turned out, he went much further than a national audience. With the French production of *Six Characters*, he gained overnight international fame.

Paradoxically, as he moves *up* toward national-cultural definition, the dramatists of the unified national literatures are moving *down* or away from a fully-conscious sense of national identity. While Pirandello aspired to bring provincial and regional theater into the large construct of a national culture, with a well-defined cultural center, the writers in Germany, France, England, and to some extent the United States were struggling to free themselves of what appeared to them as national restrictions and aiming for a supranational or international art, one that was personal and private, focused on an individualized subjectivity. It was the time of T. S. Eliot and Ezra Pound, of Brecht and Gottfried Benn:

Pirandello came to maturity during this period, when the second voice of poetry — the epic or narrative voice — and the third or dramatic voice were coming together, collapsing, into the first or monolog-lyric voice of poetry. He too focuses on the inner life, on finding the subjective correlatives for expressing that life in a lyric voice.

While playwrights like Arnolt Bronnen resort to mythical analogies (as in the grotesque Oedipal dream of *Patricide*) to find their personal and symbolic and therefore individualistic and uprooted Expressionist idiom; while Strindberg himself, late in his career, withdraws into the language of dreams and allegories; while Brecht searches for new devices that will help to find the means to articulate the message of universal brotherhood; Pirandello turns to familiar types and familiar settings, even in his most innovative plays. We are aware at all times of the special sounds and smells and habits and passions of his people, the people of Sicily, of Agrigento. Like our own Faulkner, who in his fiction succeeded in giving large utterance to human values *within* the setting of his own personal social and psychological ground, drawing for us a South full of violence and compassion, love and hate, Pirandello produces the first truly great drama which was to become the matrix for so much else outside of Italy through characterizations of the people around him, whom he knew well — shrewd overseers, passionate young men, mothers, distraught lovers, pompous government officials, tired landowners, both rich and poor, sinning women, girls in love, worldly priests, pious priests, the poor, the vulgar, the self-righteous, the silent victims of a barren land that is the symbol of death as well as love and life. Even in his last plays, the "myth" plays (*The New Colony, Lazarus, The Mountain Giants*), where he gives voice to large statements about social, religious, and artistic values, Pirandello draws his characters from the familiar, long-suffering, intense people of his native land. Through them, and in terms that are both real and suggestive of a broader application, immediate and far-reaching, he traces his ideal vision of life, a vision intensely *Italian* and at the same time transparently universal.

From the very outset Pirandello seems to have hit on a dramatic idiom that will provide the key for a new dramatic age. In *Liolâ*, written in 1916, the Sicilian environment has an Arcadian and magic quality; Liolâ and his childhood sweetheart Mita are a curious mixture of innocence and native shrewdness, victims of a rigorous system that threatens to destroy them but, at the same time, capable of turning that very system to their advantage when the claims of family and property, the reality and demands of inheritance are about to compromise their integrity. In the "theater plays" (*Six Characters, Each in His Won Way, Tonight We Improvise*), the paradoxes, inversions and "masks" of the Pirandellian stage take many shapes and forms, not the least interesting of which is the Sicilian core in each of these plays.

The empty potency of the stage — which in Pirandello is also, always, the empty potency of the Socratic self waiting to be discovered through the process of disintegration and unmasking — is expressed *in Six Characters* as the contrast between the actor's mask and the life mask, between the deficient emotional life of those outside the life experience and the unstructured intensity of the six strangers, which spills over the mold of accepted stage conventions. The actors trying to recapture the story of the six intruders, trying to translate for the stage the intense emotions of those strangers, seem colorless by comparison with the brooding dark and terrible excesses of the six characters.

In *Each In His Own Way*, the actors on stage seem unreal by comparison with the actors off stage, who are playing out the "real-life" story of their tragic affair in the lobby of the theater, during the "interludes" or "intermissions," mingling with the real audience (that is also playing a role as the stage audience needed for the scripted intermissions), bringing the action into the large context of the outside world. Here too we find intense emotions that spill beyond the stage.

In *Tonight We Improvise*, we again have a passionate Sicilian core story which, for the first time in this intriguing series of "theater plays," seems on the verge of being assimilated into the stage presentation. We sense, in this play, that the actors, unlike those in *Six Characters*, may have mastered their script: the leading actress comes so close to identifying with her role as Mommina that she actually faints, as though dead, on stage and, for a few moments, while her fellow actors puzzled and frightened gather around her, thinking she is truly ill, we too are thrust outside the play, into a wider experience.

In *Henry IV*, Pirandello gives us the resolution of the dramatic dialectic between life and the stage in a transparency which is the superimposition of many masks, a dizzying oscillation from person to non-person, staging for us the movement from a solid *one* to *no one* to a fragmented and constantly shifting self, which is never one thing, one person, one mask, but many attitudes, postures, gestures, feelings, thoughts—a variety of roles. The Sicilian "landscape" itself is "masked" in this play: we tend to overlook it as we move within the fiction of an 11th century "emperor" living in a mansion made into a castle to suit his role-playing. But in fact the core story here too is intensely Sicilian, embedded as it were, in other times and fictions.

The measure of Pirandello's commitment to the psychological, social, and religious realities of his native environment may be found in a comparison between *Henry IV* (1922) and his late novel, *One, No One, and A Hundred Thousand* (1925). The novel (reminiscent in many ways of James Joyce's *Ulysses*) deals with the same kind of phenomenon found in *Henry IV*: the infinite reflections of self. In both works identity is a layering of masks, glimpses caught of oneself, mirrored images — literal ones in the novel; historical and psychological ones in the play. In both instances, the protagonist's insistence on finding his true self verges on *obsession* — what others see as *madness*.

In his early novel, *The Late Mattia Pascal* (1903), the first clear statement of the disintegration of personality, which was to become the burden of his plays (triggered in this case by the wrong identification of a body found drowned), Pirandello has one of his characters explain the transformation of ancient into modern tragedy with this ingenious image of a puppet show of the tragedy of Orestes:

> Now listen to this crazy notion that just came to me! Let's suppose that at the very climax, when the puppet who represents Orestes is about to take his revenge on Aegisthus and his mother for his father's death, a great hole were suddenly torn in the paper sky of the theater, what would happen? . . . Orestes would still be bent on revenge, he would still be impatient to bring it about, but his eyes in that instant would be directed up there, to that ripped sky, where all kinds of evil influences would now filter down into the scene, and he would feel his arms grow limp. Orestes, in other words, would become Hamlet. The whole difference, Signor Meis, between ancient and modern tragedy, is just that, believe me: a hole in the paper sky.[4]

That hole in the paper sky has produced not only Hamlet but, by extension, the fragmented personalities of Pirandello's stage. What has filtered down are all the humors of the soul, the inexpressible and often contradictory impulses of the idiosyncratic character, drawn in their Sicilian realism with the universal lyric voice of the poet.

In staging the dialectic of personal identity, which often ends with the protagonists rushing off into the darkness, which is also the darkness of the soul,

Pirandello — as Robert Brustein observes —dramatizes "the very act of creation." His *dramatis personae* are the living signatures of his artistry, "being both his product and his process."[5] His open-ended plays remind us that the familiar characters we are watching, rooted in a clearly defined landscape, are also images of a larger picture in which we, the audience — and not just the Italian audience — must also assume roles. This is especially evident in the "theater plays."

There is always in the particularized settings of Pirandello's plays, the suggestion of a larger vista in which the stage action and the audience response come together, the real stage and the life stage blend into a single experience; in which the play forces the audience to be more than spectators. In *Six Characters*, the audience in immediately drawn into the action as the six strangers interrupt a rehearsal in an empty theater — for just beyond the footlights is a full theater with an audience watching what is going on — the suggestion of a Chinese-box arrangement, underscored in *Each in His Own Way* and made explicit in *Tonight We Improvise*. In this connection it is also interesting to recall that in the "theater plays" the "real-life" drama overwhelms the "stage drama" in every case. *Henry IV* is the ingenious superimposition of the particular and the universal — the layering of time and action, of past and present, of old and new, of pageants and real life, of portraits and living people and fictional characters, all rising out of a local event.

This dramatic dialectic is present in the short plays as well. *The License* is an intense dramatic but also humorous statement about prejudice, in this case the Sicilian belief in the "evil eye," and the notion that those who have it are like "carriers" of a dreadful disease, to be avoided at all costs. The protagonist, Chiarchiaro, and his entire family have become virtual outcasts, shunned by the villagers because of the bad luck they've suffered, through no fault of their own. No one will hire any of them, they are destitute. Driven to despair, Chiarchiaro hits on an ingenious scheme: he will bring a libel suit against the Mayor's son, not to win but to lose the case. Once the verdict has been handed down against him, he will have calling cards made with his "official" title as a carrier of the "evil eye." He will earn his living and support his family by visiting the stores every day, leaving his calling card with the proprietor and standing in the doorway until the owner pays him to move on and his clients feel free to enter without danger of "contagion."

In *Right You Are! (If You Think So)*, we face a similar situation in the gossip and biases of a provincial town, small enough for people to know (or get to know) everything that's going on. Here too the characters are drawn from Pirandello's familiar Sicilian world.

On a "protocol" call to her son-in-law's new employer, Councilman Agazzi, Signora Frola, seems to anticipate the man's questions and launches quickly into an explanation about the unusual living arrangements Signore Ponza has made and which have caused so much gossip. She tells Agazzi and the others with him that Ponza believes his first wife, Signora Frola's daughter, died and that he has remarried since. The truth is, she goes on, the girl recovered, but Ponza insisted it was not his wife and a mock ceremony had to be performed before he would take her back, as his "second" wife. Now overly protective, he insists that no one come close to the girl, not even her own mother, Signora Frola, who has been installed in an elegant apartment just down the hall from Agazzi's, while he and his wife have settled in a walk-up on the edge of town, a good distance away. Her listeners are stunned.

On the heels of Signora Frola's departure, Ponza shows up with a very different story. His mother-in-law, he explains, had lapsed into a deep depression when her daughter died. Then, one day she happened to see him from the window of the home where she had been recovered, strolling with his new wife, and concluded that her daughter had recovered and was back with her husband. Her "delusion" brought about a complete recovery. Ponza has allowed her the fiction, but to make sure that the two women never get close enough for Signora Frola to realize the truth and fall ill again, he has forbidden her to climb to the top floor to visit with his wife. The two women communicate by exchanging notes in a basket that is raised and lowered.

Soon after, Signora Frola rushes back to the Aguzzis a second time, fully aware of what Ponza has been telling them and anxious to set things right. She assures them that she is not mad; that it is Ponza who is suffering under the delusion that his wife died. She allows the fiction, she tells them and — much as it pains her — keeps from climbing up to visit with her daughter because Ponza is obsessively protective. . . .

All subsequent efforts to get at the truth fail, because the town from which Ponza and the women came has been completely leveled by a massive earthquake that destroyed everything, including government offices and the documents stored in them. To put a stop finally to all the rumors, Agazzi orders Ponza to bring in his wife: surely the woman can tell them who she is? But when she arrives, heavily veiled, all she says, in answer to the crucial question, is "I am who you think I am."

Critics have used this particular line to prove, mistakenly, that Pirandello is a relativist. He is, in fact, asserting the opposite. Both Signore Ponza and Signora Frola have accepted, without any shred of doubt, the conviction that sustains them, the internal certainty of their faith. To the others, who have relied on external "facts" for the truth, who have been frustrated in those terms, the veiled woman will always be a mystery.

These examples should suffice to show how Pirandello draws for us, with the lightest touch, a crowd of human possibilities and educates us to deal with them. In the final pages of his "Introduction to the Italian Theater," he dismisses the realistic theater that prevailed, that had deteriorated into "sheer entertainment" and predicts a glorious new age for the Italian theater, which was once again exerting its influence on the world — the regional drama of Milan, Venice, Naples, Sicily,

> by means of which our theatrical productions, too, move in the great current of that constant reaction against intellectualism that is, after all, one of the greatest contributions of our genius to civilization; that, finally, after the long quest of the last century, the movement of our new Theater led happily and suddenly to the discovery of a virgin field, particularly suited to our dramatic talent, and found a true voice for the expression of new conflicts, abandoning all psychological study or indulgence, all normative aims, in order to realize without further ado the direct and free expression of those genuine emotions that are present and striving in the soul of every man, without fear of the contradictions that prevail in the emotional life, in the imagination, and in the will — contradictions that, until then, had been scrupulously avoided as incapable of being assimilated within the moral and aesthetic integrity of the character. Out of this came, indirectly, the most caustic criticism of contemporary society ever articulated by writers of any age. It was nothing less than an illumination of the psychological state of man in our time and it was recognized at once as characteristic and true, not only of the Italian soul, but also of our universal culture, in all those countries of the world that share in it. This explains the expansive force of the new Italian Theater, which has brought substance and spirit back into the work of so many European and American dramatists, directing their art to that vast virgin world of the unexplored life of human personality: something for which the creative artists of our time evidently must have felt a pressing need, since with the first suggestion provided by our creative, original Italians, those others — almost to a man — have turned to confront that world with the most varied means and from the most diverse spiritual points of view.[6]

This description of a revitalized Italian theater that portrays the paradox of human emotions, that had already led European and American dramatists into "that vast virgin world of the unexplored life of human personality" is, in fact, a fitting description of Pirandello's own theater. Implicit in all his innovations, in his incredible variety of characters and settings, at the very core of his drama, is the awareness that the Sicilian voices that resonate in all his plays are, in the end, the universal monolog-lyric voice of the dramatist himself, who has translated the particulars of experience into a universal language with solid roots in the national culture.

NOTES

1. The voice of drama, according to T. S. Eliot, who acknowledged his debt to the Hegelian Expressionist poet/critic, Gottfried Benn. See, T. S. Eliot, "The Three Voices of Poetry," *On Poets and Poetry* (Noonday Press, New York, 1943, etc.), pp. 96, 112.

2. Anne and Henry Paolucci, "Dante and the 'Quest For Eloquence" in India's Vernacular Languages," *Review of National Literatures*, Vol. 10 *India*, (Council on National Literatures, New York, 1980), pp. 70-144.

3. T S. Eliot, "American Literature and the American Language," *To Criticize the Critic* (New York, 1965), p. 54.

4. Anne Paolucci, *Pirandello's Theater: The Recovery of the Modern Stage for Dramatic Art* (Southern Illinois University Press, Carbondale, 1974; rptd Griffon House Publications, Smyrna DE, 2002), p. 1.

5. *Ibid.*, p. 5.

6. "Pirandello's Introduction to the Italian Theater," translated by Anne Paolucci, *Genius of the Italian Theater*, ed. Eric Bentley (Mentor Books/New American Library, New York, 1964), pp. 11-29.

"Pirandello's Introduction to the Italian Theater"
(Translated by Anne Paolucci)

It is difficult for us to realize the importance of the Theater in the civic life of a people, after having sat through the usual sort of play being offered the public these days — and not only here in Italy.

I ask you, therefore, to return in thought to the times when truly civilized human societies — such as existed in ancient Greece and Rome, and, as far as we know, much earlier in India, and later, during the Renaissance, in Rome again but above all in Ferrara and in our own thriving Florence — celebrated the Theater as a religious or quasi-religious rite; as a genuinely "vital act" that united all the spectators in a reality expressly created by the poet to exalt their feelings.

One could then still feel, almost palpably, what the Theater in its innermost essence really is: a form of life itself, existing even among lower animals who, through irrational, are yet capable of playing and offering their play as a spectacle for others; and much more among men, who in their instinctive need to see themselves in action are moved to represent their own lives, to judge and thereby understand themselves better in relation to others — that is, before the immediate sense of a Whole, of which they rightly think and feel themselves to be inseparable parts, component elements. Out of such natural necessity the Theater is born among all peoples. It is born when a people sing joyfully or tearfully in religious feasts and one among them rises, exalted or grieving, to commemorate a god or a hero, the rest attending him

---

Originally published as the Introduction to Genius *of the Italian Theatre, ed. Eric Bentley (Mentor Books/New American Library, 1964) pp. 11-29.*

in chorus, and then two or three or more separate themselves from the crowd to personify, in a truly authentic representation, punctuated by the measured sequences of the chorus, the fortunate or tragic adventures of the god or hero.

That one might do without Theater was then inconceivable. Every year there came a day — and more than once each year — when Theater was the solemn fulfillment, not so much of the particular day, as of a longed-for and necessary expression of communal life, an example which that life offered itself; and the word of the poet found its place much more visibly among the highest ideal values of those human societies.

But someone will say: those societies are not ours, which is so much more civilized, so much more vast and complex; and, on the other hand, the Theater of those times is a far cry from ours, which has become, alas, so much tinier, so much more futile and — we might almost say — useless. In that vast complex of values that is the civilized nation of today, what importance can there be in a representation of the fictitious adventures of an amateur detective trying to unmask a criminal in the least suspect character of a comedy?

Today the Theater can be no more than the pastime of an evening for persons who, having worked all day, want to enjoy some honest relaxation before going to bed.

And who might these persons be, who, having worked all day, can still have the desire, the time, and the means to relax after dinner at the Theater before going to bed?

Can we honestly say they are "the people"? — "the Community"?

No. Only some few from the wealthy and middle classes, and an occasional businessman.

Let us at once admit, therefore, that if it ever had great value in the life of a people, if it was ever capable of having such great value, the Theater has lost it today; it is no longer performed for the people as a whole, nor, in conscience, would it be worthy of such performance, in its present state. Today it is merely a pastime, and less entertaining than many other pastimes.

Admittedly, this seems to be what we call a realistic argument, one that accepts facts as they are, stripped of rhetorical embellishments, and draws the inevitable conclusions — ugly and wretched as they are — calling a spade a spade. Instead, it is a cheap sophism, a sop for that miserable instinct of lazy indifference with which we have allowed ourselves to regard things of the spirit, responding momentarily with enthusiasm only when they are blatantly presented to us with the pressing enticements of rhetoric.

Reasoning about it with intellectual honesty, one is bound to see that the Theater today has not lost, and could not have lost, any of its real value, because that value is an intrinsic part of its very nature and, therefore, impossible to lose. What a people, coming en masse to the solemn spectacles of religious feasts, made of the Theater in the past — that is, a vital, communal act of the highest spiritual value — the Theater today, in and for itself, by its own virtue, insofar as it is truly Theater, makes of its audience, howsoever composed, howsoever sparse. What I mean to say is that when, in a half-empty hall, before a few scattered spectators, a real work of art is presented, those few, that evening, by virtue of that magic power which poetry acquires when its characters take on flesh and come to life on the stage, have become nothing more or less than "the People." And so much the worse for whoever stayed away; he missed the chance to participate in an experience of spiritual life actually and wholly realized within the circle of the community of which he is a part, and there can be nothing to boast of in his having turned his back to it.

But what in essence is the Theater? What is that value which is intrinsic to it and which, therefore, can never be lost?

I spoke of it on a recent occasion and I repeat it now in the same words: by giving voice to feelings and thoughts which are altogether evident in the lively play of passions represented, and which because of the very nature of this art form, have to be spelled out in terms as clear and precise as possible, the Theater offers what might properly be called a public trial of human actions as they truly are, in that pure and everlasting reality which the imagination of poets creates as an example and warning for our commonplace and confused natural life — a trial both free and human, which spurs the conscience of the judges themselves to an ever loftier and more rigorous moral life. This, in my judgment, is the value of the Theater; and I wanted to state it in advance to assure you that in undertaking now to speak of the first and foremost Theater of the world, which is the Italian, we are dealing with a serious matter.

I fear, let me admit, that someone among you may have marveled at my saying "the first and foremost Theater of the world, which is the Italian." My hope is that, after reading these pages of mine, marvel will give way in his spirit to a less prejudicial and more considerate regard for the ideal values of which even he, as an Italian, is a depository — established values renewed and augmented, age after age, by those who shaped this great nation of ours.

The time has come to make amends, good people, even in this area, for that damnable pleasure we take in disparaging the value of our own things and belittling them in comparison with their foreign counterparts. After so many centuries of indulgence, that damnable pleasure has become a sort of comfortable niche for spiritual indolence and a cheap excuse for personal and collective irresponsibility regarding these values, which instead of accepting we rejected so as not to have to defend and preserve them later — an attitude which, prior to that most sacred renewal of public life brought on by Fascism, could well be considered one of the characteristic traits (among the least attractive) of the Italians. And it must be acknowledged, painfully, that perhaps the only ones immune to it were our humble peasants and artisans, who, as often as circumstances matched them against foreign peasants and artisans, felt and knew and had the heart to declare themselves openly to be superior to the others, more skillful, more capable of work; while our "intelligentsia," in the schools, in the newspapers, in books, in conversations, in spirit, out of intellectual poverty, out of narrow-mindedness, often out of ignorance, always for want of conscience (for that is what the absence of right judgment, true culture, and broad sensibility amount to in matters involving personal responsibility), took pleasure in ridiculing, with polished skepticism, every genuinely Italian literary expression: or, when ridicule was out of the question, took similar pleasure in hedging on their dutiful concession of meager praise by searching breathlessly to discover, as a necessary justification, where, why, and to what extent — granted it was a beautiful thing, a beautiful comedy, for example — we might at least consider it somewhat French . . . or, if French is really out of the question, at least somewhat German, or, desperately, for want of anything better, at least somewhat English: there! for it is always possible to detect a Shakespearean influence whenever there is an elevation of tone in any of our theatrical works, beginning with those of the fifteenth and sixteenth centuries which Shakespeare — fortunately for him— knew so well. Well worth his knowing! And were they not also familiar to Molière and Calderon, and Lope de Vega? Vivacious, loquacious. bursting with strange and picaresque experiences just then gained in an adventuresome world all their own, they revealed all their secrets to extremely attentive ears. . . .

But we must not anticipate. It might be worthwhile, first of all, to recall a point of fact, which is, in fact, a point of time.

The European Theater is not really as old as, in its confused totality, it may appear to one who neglects to verify the chronology of his facts. The medieval Theater is, for a long stretch of time, a desert in which every now and then, instead of an oasis of life, we may come upon, at most, some tiny place where the only vestiges of human existence are a few squalid tombs — never a mausoleum. What I mean is, there is actually nothing for centuries, and when, at rare intervals, we do find something, it is a stillborn babe. There was much talk, at one time, about the poetess-nun Roswitha, as if hers were a living voice coming to us out of that darkness; but, really, even hers is a voice of death, resounding coldly out of a poor shriveled corpse laid to rest in its final peace. Much time has yet to go by before we hear in Italy — while a few learned scholars announce with a thrill of excitement the glorious recovery of Seneca, in the midst of the fresh prattling of the new sweet-sounding language — a first living voice, a voice that is no longer artificial, no longer pitched to the timbre of a sepulchral tradition, a voice from human hearts overflowing with emotion, a *present* voice, revealing and vitalizing an age that appears to be inhabited, at long last, by a new people, moving with ease in the intimacy of their homes, at work, in their fields, gathered together to pray in their churches. And indeed it seems as if the world of man were revived in an act of prayer of boundless gratitude for the beautiful sun of Italy that warms and illuminates it. The place where for the first time Christ finally moves like a living person among men, a sign of heartfelt faith, a voice of poetry resounding from the heart and no longer a dogmatic formula mouthed in an already forgotten language, the place where Christ appears as the first sublime character of the Theater of the new Christian world, is Italy. Here the fancy of ingenuous poets makes Him talk, as a man, with the Madonna, His Mother, and the Saints — and as He talks with them, all coldness is thawed, the infinite distance between earth and heaven having given way.

A great mental deafness has heretofore afflicted our learned professors of literary history, who presume to compare the contemporary *mistères* of France — in which the inner spirit does not yet move or give even the slightest sign of disentangling itself from the abstract rigidity of medieval intellectualism — with our vitally human expressions of Umbrian devotion.

Expansive warmth as opposed to sententiousness; spontaneous turns, ingenuousness of surprise and discoveries as opposed to an almost impassive repetition of formulas hardly capable of anything other than a slight variation of words — this is what they should have felt, in that comparison; they might then have been prevented from committing so lightheartedly that offense against truth, that offense against ourselves, which we find in the so-called impartiality with which, one after the other, in their textbooks and manuals, they repeat monotonously, "Contemporaneous with that of the French *mistères* was the development of our own Umbrian devotions," and stop there.

The essential vitality of this first dramatic expression of ours is clearly revealed to us by the way it eventually develops into the organic complexity of the sacred representations of the Passion, or as the Christian legends associated with this or that saint, which are and will remain imperishable artistic monuments of the natural religious birth of the Italian Theater.

It is a rare pleasure to notice how this religious poetry — guided by a sure instinct to appropriate the boldest expressions of dramatic narrative and the purest of the lyric, upon which all truly theatrical language is founded and sustained — from another point of view (that is, with respect to what we might call content), takes nourishment, in its thirst for a human element, from the purest sources, such as seem to conform least with its religious nature but are in fact most suited to give it the warmth and movement of life, and with that, the possibility of art: and for that very reason, a genuine power to uplift human hearts.

Having given present-day life to those great Personalities whose acts and feelings it exalts as an example and comfort to men and no longer merely as an abstract exercise in rendering praise, it surrounds them with an assembly of other living personalities of the time, who, in the background of the mythical action, retain their first and last names, their habits, their inner world, and all those limitations that serve to define personalities. The poet thus has discovered for himself the same device of the painter, who, on the altarpiece commissioned of him, depicts his pious patron kneeling in the midst of his family and friends, the curate of the church, the hunting dog, capturing them in gestures and expressions of daily life — the dog barking and frightening the baby, the mother comforting it in her arms, the neighbor anxiously gesturing for silence lest the absorption of the *paterfamilias* in his adoration of the Sacred Images be disturbed; and these Images, alive, breathing the same air, but not otherwise embodied or dressed than the human figure, glow nevertheless with greater beauty, nobility, and grace. This alone distinguishes them from the figures drawn from life, raises them above the others, guards them against all earthy baseness, in an aura of happiness that seems to derive from their own surpassing beauty — the only evidence the artist is now able to supply of their divine essence.

It is the bursting forth of life within a confining pattern. The professor of literature — his own mind a series of rigid patterns — will see in all this nothing more than naiveté, absence of logic, crudeness; and to spare himself the subtle irritation of things not understood, he will dismiss them as "crude aspects of popular art," to discourse leisurely, instead, on the "regular forms," those aspects of culture where one may hope to find more seriousness, a greater sense of responsibility.

But, alas, the Italian Theater is not a field for professors of literary history. Incredible as it might sound, they do not succeed in understanding even the "regular forms," as they call them. For these forms, although deriving, for tragedy, from classical imitation of Seneca (and later, with the Greek renaissance, from imitation of Aeschylus, Sophocles, and Euripides), and for comedy, from Plautus and Terence, nevertheless — how shall I say? — can hardly be called serious: they, too, insist on exposing themselves to the contamination of life, and with the same crude arrogance of the sacred representations force their classical pattern to accommodate a mass of characters never encountered before, dangerously uneducated, involved in the strangest intrigues.

The evidence is irresistible: both the sacred representations and the imitations of Classical Tragedy, both popular art and cultured art, have inexplicably absorbed something that seems made of air, and inflates them, and makes new characters breathe in them.

What can it be?

But it's obvious: it is our very life, newly conceived; our new substance, unadulterated and altogether original; our new life as it appears in the tales of Boccaccio.

It is the spirit of romance.

The Italian Theater could not have originated otherwise than by absorbing this spirit of romance, already alive in another of our literary forms, which had become, one might say, a daily household reality among us. But we must insist: among us only; as we must also insist that the European Theater at this time is still something far off, yet to come. And this is understandably so, for even the European Theater, when it arrives, will have as its sole substance that same spirit of romance, which is *ours*, undeniably *ours*; and it will have to wait for our Theater to provide it.

Try to imagine what this spirit of romance must have meant to a world grown incapable of detaching itself from intellectual concepts. It meant life: it meant liberation from the tyranny of a mind grown subtle, made constantly more pointed, abstract, and dry by its mania for logical distinctions. Opening the heart to the spirit of romance will be like depriving logic of voice and passing it on to the imagination. And thus we see men of sheer intellect rediscovering that they have senses: legs that can carry them to far-off countries, and eyes and ears with which to see and hear true and strange and wholly unexpected things, which discourage any attempt to probe for syllogisms and must be drawn simply for what they are — adventures. So many adventures! How complicated human affairs have suddenly become! If we remember the sort of complications — intellectual complications — that until then men had been used to, we realize at once the reason for that farrago of interconnected, entangled, crowded happenings of the sacred representations, which have us almost breathless.

Now, it is in Italy, in the tales of Boccaccio, that this spirit of romance manifests itself for the first time as wholly free, content within itself, heedless of all else. To provide the impetus for the modern Theater, to become a suitable leaven for such a development, it had first to discard completely all its old traits of intellectualistic exemplarism (retaining which — and this is a necessary distinction — even if present elsewhere, as in the French *fabliaux*, that spirit could serve no real purpose since it remained merely an instrument of ratiocination). And, having acquired the magic of life in its objective reality through the creative genius of the great Boccaccio — the true father *ante literam* of the humanistic renaissance in the still medieval European world — it had next to find someone to lift and carry it, in its entirety, from the novella (which is like the mirror of one solitary consciousness placed before another, silent, consciousness, that of the reader) into the Theater — that is, into the midst of social life, which by its very nature is bound to respect all conventions, including literary ones. It is natural for such emancipation to take place first in isolated individuals, in those of keenest sensibilities, while society as a whole is still tied down by its ancient rules and, though secretly desiring it, fears all that is new, believing itself incapable of controlling it, should it accept such novelty in its midst. Who will take on the task? Who will accomplish, with the Theater, this decisive test of strength?

Italian society, with the Italian Theater.

It will come into being as soon as it is possible and *insofar* as it is possible to represent in action, without narrative supports and before popular audiences, those new, thoroughly human, and romantic adventures that already were being felt in our midst, above all among the common people. This change takes place among us as a spontaneous and happy one, on a popular level. Once it has taken place, the task is accomplished: everyone now can see how it is done. And the European Theater has been shown the way.

The germ and many of the subsequent stages of growth of the modern European Theater are already present in our sacred representations.

Among us, the discovery brings, from the very first moment, such a sense of relief that we feel an impulse to be humorous even in the company of saints; and the comic is freely introduced into the sacred representations. The lesson will be used to advantage by Shakespeare, later.

Divine providence — called thus so long as it governed every detail of a life incapable of movement — relaxes the chains of its absolute governance, reveals itself often enough as chance, blindly agitating mortal creatures, and as fortune, thrusting them into all sorts of adventures; and only in the happy or tragic ending of the representation does it come again to be considered the polar star by whose light — but as an afterthought only — a moral is drawn regarding all that happened among these people left thus almost entirely on their own, guided in their conduct by natural ethics rather than precepts, by sentiment rather than the constraints of reverential fear. Lope and Calderon will make use of all this to give vigor and movement and human excitement to their religious dramas.

Considering the importance of the result attained, the time required will not seem excessive: with the sacred representations, we find ourselves beyond the second half of the fifteenth century, well into the sixteenth; and yet the suggestive power of expression in these masterworks of ours, the sheer intensity of their tragic and lyric motifs, still retain the ingenuous freshness of the beginning. Indeed, that same spirit of romance out of which they were born made possible, two centuries later, an almost miraculous revival in them, or rather a second flowering, of our fourteenth century. It is a new test. And interestingly enough, many who rely more on the promptings of their own sensibilities than on dates take them actually to be works of the fourteenth century; while some learned scholar who, instead, relies heavily on dates and external evidence will begin to suspect that the ingenuous, frank representation of Saint Uliva, which enchanted and edified us all a short time ago, might well be a late work — as late, perhaps, as the sixteenth century. He is probably right; but so are we in saying: fourteenth century.

In the light of this esthetic intuition, which for me is beyond all doubt and which rests, after all, on abundant factual evidence, we can assert with complete conviction that the culminating outburst of the Theater, in all Europe, in the seventeenth century — Shakespeare in England, Lope and Calderon in Spain, Molière in France — is a direct outgrowth of the Italian matrix. Molière alone was frank enough to admit: *"je prends mon bien où je le trouve,"* in answer to those who remarked that perhaps he had gone too far in appropriating not only situations and characters but entire scenes from our *commedia dell'arte*; and he was right in shrugging off such remarks, considering the narrow point of view reflected in them. The truth is that all these great authors, these originators of the

European Theater, had appropriated — without being aware of it — something quite different: the very sp[irit of our Theater.

The Theater seemed to them to be the only original and living form of expression from which one could take his bearings; just as today, of all the works of that time, only theirs seem original to us. A perfectly natural attitude, then as now, for the awareness of originality is much clearer, much more compelling in connection with foreign works; while a much more cultivated taste is required to recognize it in our own writings, in which the greater their originality, the more unassuming their appearance. To those on familiar terms with them they seem perfectly natural and not especially noteworthy. Do we ever make a fuss over the plain, ordinary drinking water we use every day? But no sooner do we move to another town, and water, than we notice the change in taste. Now, the specialist in literary history ought to be able to distinguish it with unerring precision; he should have, in other words, an esthetic taste so cultivated as to enable him to recognize, in the unassuming plainness that seems so natural, the vital originality of certain works. And should he have the good fortune of discovering such a work in his own backyard, so to speak, he ought to publicize it, acknowledging its true value and studying carefully the things around it, both near and far, to determine just how, where, and when its appearance changed and directed subsequent artistic activity.

Reputations have first of all to be established at home. And that of the Italian Theater suffers from the fact that those who first concerned themselves with it failed, from the very outset, to recognize the new values which that Theater was bringing into the world. Attention was regularly diverted from those works, as being merely "popular," that is, of no account (on the basis of God only knows what distorted values and tasteless prejudices); and there was chronic complaining over the alleged ruin wrought by classical imitation in what the professors call the "regular" forms — forms which, on the contrary, immediately expanded to admit the popular element, so that they too absorbed and made their own the spirit of romance, reflecting all the contingent interests of the society of the time. The very trunkline of our Theater was thus neglected; as a consequence, its history must be retraced from the beginning, in order to credit it with the enormous importance it once had and still has.

What was missed, to be perfectly clear, was the very essence of the development of our Theater.

Why, and how, does the *Commedia dell'arte* come into being?

The assignment of so much weight — so much crushing weight — to the imitations of Latin and Greek models in order to justify a hasty and utterly stupid condemnation of them (a condemnation by no means applicable solely to the products of the Italian Theater) served, on the one hand, merely to conceal the true value of what was lively and timely in those classicizing works, and, on the other, to give a semblance of authority to that paradoxical notion that, of all people, we who had rediscovered the humanistic spirit in the recovered masterpieces of the classical world had made use of these only as literary models and academic exercises. Nothing of the sort ever happened, except in the minds of our professors of literary history. Classical forms had anything but a stifling effect on Poliziano's *Orfeo;* Buonarroti the Younger remained untouched by them in his teeming and popularesque *Fiera* and *Tancia*; while that spirited rough hewer of types and scenes, Giovan Maria Cecchi, and the great Machiavelli in that masterpiece which is the *Mandragola*, profited greatly from a liberal use of hese forms, as Aretino also did, and Ariosto, whose *Negromante* should be considered, in the final analysis, not as a descendant of those Latin models but as the primogenitor of *Tartuffe* and *Rabagas*; until, finally, the boundless, irrepressible humor of Giordano

Bruno's *Candelaio*, altogether shattered them, preannouncing the coming of romanticism — and all this in the course of little more than a century. But in those same sixteenth and seventeenth centuries an entirely different current of popular Theater was also running its course. There, by the side of a nobleman like Alioni d'Aste, who observes and describes in his farces the manners of the lower classes, or the *litterati* of the Neapolitan court, who do the same in their farces about the people of Cava de' Tirreni, we begin to run into the type of theatrical personality who is at once author, actor, and producer of comic works: Ruzzante, first and foremost, whose works, translated into French by Mortier, won new acclaim a few years ago through the efforts of Jacques Copeau; the Sienese artisans of the *Accademia dei Rozzi*, celebrated for their rustic farces, which they were invited to perform at the court of Ferrara as well as that of the Pope; the Neapolitan school of comedy, out of which a little later came the remarkable production of Antonio della Porta; the Venetian Andrea Calmo, who began to introduce local dialects in his many comedies; finally, Andreini, who tours half of Europe with his famous troupes and, gifted with a solid talent and high ambitions, writes, in addition to licentious farces, sacred dramas of vast design.

The *Commedia dell'arte* emerged little by little, precisely from theatrical personalities such as these, who, as actors, knew the pulse of the public and, as authors, also indulged their own personal tastes and ambitions; thus Ruzzante was drawn, for example, to the naïve world of the fields, while Colmo was attracted by that crucible of races and interests that was Venice. But they were also well acquainted with the output of the *litterati*, and as producers took out options on those works, performing them with their own, or revising them to suit their purposes. It is absurd to imagine in this an accidental discovery of mere actors. Anyone having even the slightest acquaintance with the way an actor works on stage, with the precise directions he requires if he is to take a step to the right instead of the left, will readily see that the idea of improvising their performances could never have occurred to actors.

The *Commedia dell'arte* is born, on the contrary, out of authors who are so deeply involved in the theater, in the life of the Theater, as to become, in fact, actors; who begin by writing the comedies they later perform, comedies at once more theatrical because not written in the isolated study of the man of letters but in the presence, as it were, of the warm breath of the public; who then take up the task of adapting for their own performance and that of their troupe the comedies of other authors, old and new, in order to supply the pressing need for repertory, constantly revising these adaptations, after having tried out on their audiences the effectiveness of certain flourishes added as an outlet and vehicle for the particular talents of some actor of the company. And as their fellow actors gradually become skilled in keeping up the already-familiar repartee of the middle episodes, they will write only the exits and the outline of the action.

In other words, those authors must have lost all their serious artistic pretensions: the transitory, impassioned life of the Theater must have taken such full possession of them that the only interest left to them was that of the spectacle itself — a complete absorption in the quality of the performance and communication with the audience.

They are no longer authors; but they are no longer even actors, in the true sense of the word.

What are they, then?

By now each one of them has become a *type*, with a completely defined stage life of its own; so that finally a theatrical convention is established whereby with ten of them, ten such types — no more, no less — a complex and varied spectacle can be put on that will provide full satisfaction for the audience — an audience already familiar with these conventions, with the rules of the game, and passionately interested in how their favorites carry on, how far each succeeds in giving prominence to his part.

And where do these types come from?

That ancient ambition of authorship which had spurred Ruzzante, for example, to write his bitter comedies gradually wore itself down, turning from the creation of an entire comedy to the creation, or rather to the recopying of one of its characters, that of the country bumpkin, at once simple and shrewd: Zanni. And the figure thus made his entrance into a world no longer his own; out of his natural element, he found himself, still in his characteristic tight-fitting clothes, on the bare boards of a stage during the performance . . . of a comedy about somebody else! One by one the rest of these figures, or — at this point — the rest of these types, found themselves on the same stage in the same predicament. And the comedies from which they had come were also there together on the stage: all . . . and none. For, that passionate love of the Theater that wanted to see them all exhibited there together had dried up their vital sap, thus destroying their form. What remained, concentrated in those types, was their sheer movement.

It was now a question of reducing all these movements into some kind of order. These various types, each distinguished in its unmistakable dress and speech — here, with Zanni, is Pantalon de' Bisognosi, and with them, the terrible Capitano, and Arlecchino and Brighella and Doctor Balanzon and the little maidservant and the pining sweetheart and the gallant cavalier — had now to be assigned a role in some sort of intrigue within a more or less logical pattern of development which the classical forms, long emptied of their comedy, easily provided.

It is impossible to conceive of greater contempt for the classical literary world on the part of those who first brought it to light, those same people whose creative powers — the professors of literary history would have us believe — were paralyzed and suffocated, with regard to the Theater, precisely by imitation of those models.

We who have recovered from them what was living and restored it to the world were also the ones who, very early, transformed their characters into types so that the labor of sterile imitation might not be prolonged *ad infinitum*: transformed into types, they continued to provide entertainment — for us and for the entire world.

Only Italy, with its Theater, can thus boast of having drained the recovered classical world of all that it had to offer.

Because of the exceptional skill of its traveling comics (the so-called *improvvisi*), the *Commedia dell'arte* — which as we have seen, was perhaps a more vulgar and practical, perhaps a quicker and more prudent way, certainly a more decisive way, of profiting from all the material of classical comedy (something which the literary writers, in other ways and for other reasons, were themselves striving for) — enjoyed universal acclaim and throughout that entire period was regarded, outside of Italy, as synonymous with the Italian Theater itself. Meanwhile, perhaps to console somewhat the professors of literary history, Tasso was creating that admittedly Italian but also undeniably literary genre: the pastoral drama. In it, those who cannot feel the power of the Theater may enjoy themselves at leisure with the harmony of the verse and other such charms and, after much waiting, may expect as much of quite another kind of esthetic enjoyment from the delicately ornate dramas of Metastasio, where, one cannot resist saying, the poetry is genuine enough and superabundant, but the Theater has slipped out through the service entrance.

With the *Commedia dell'arte*, on the contrary, our Theater led the way — in France, especially, but also in England and Spain. It emerged triumphant in its aggressive vitality wherever the local Theater, not having covered the same course as ours, still lingered in pure and simple imitation of those classical models that we already had reconsidered, and struggled vainly to infuse new life into those very forms that we, instead, had rid ourselves of, to experiment freely and impetuously with all the theatrical movement that could be gotten from them.

In life, a spirit of romance; in the Theater, a sense of movement.

This was the definitive and timely lesson that our Theater offered the European Theater; nor can we complain of the students who made us of it. Shortly thereafter, we find among the graduates of that same school our own Goldoni.

Here, too, our literary histories seem to be apologizing that the Italian Theater, having reached at last the possibility of bringing forth a great author, should have give us, with Goldoni, simply a minor version of Molière,

Here again we have failed to recognize the novelty and originality of our own native works. Goldoni is rightly celebrated, of course, for having relaxed the rigidity of the masks in their strained and artificial laughter and for having reanimated the now flexible muscles of the human face with the natural laughter of a life caught in the midst of the most vivacious and, at the same time, most exquisite and incomparably graceful activity. But the vitality of his creations, entrusted for all time to the first direct and natural language ever to be spoken on the stage, does not spring from the fact that he has given new form, human form, to the movement of masks and types of the *Commedia dell'arte:* that had been marvelously done by both Shakespeare and Molière. The effort had transformed types into characters. And we will never discover the true Goldoni if we fix our attention on the characters that, according to the fashion of the time, he too, tried to create — the good-natured boor, the grumbler, the miser, etc. They are indeed marvelous; but in the comedies in which they appear as protagonists the truly great new author reveals himself, on the contrary, in the subordinate characters, one of whom — the little housemaid, for example — suddenly becomes, like Mirandolina, the center of a comedy of her own; and many others come forward, en masse, to stand there and bicker freely in the streets of Chioggia.

What has happened?

Simply this: the Theater has taken, unexpectedly, such a long leap forward that it can hardly believe it, and for a time, beginning with Gozzi, it will try, in its confusion, to turn back.

Goldoni has transcended "character," and has seized — with an unapproachable facility, with an astounding lightness of touch — all the volubility, the fluidity, the contradiction, the spontaneity of life in action, and has thus, with the stroke of a magic wand, opened the way for the contemporary Theater to come streaming forth out of the massive rock in which the "characters" of the seventeenth century had been rough-hewn, not yet great, as they appear to us now, but simply big.

At this point, having seen how false it is to hold that the Italian Theater before Goldoni was simply a desert or cemetery, and having touched briefly upon (what surely deserves a fuller discussion) the true greatness of Goldoni's genius, which is far greater than we Italians as a rule acknowledge it to be, I would like to talk about the grave sin we commit in allowing such riches to lie inert and forgotten — riches which, if taken up boldly with a revitalizing spirit altogether legitimate in the Theater, would constitute our glory and prestige in this field.

The Theater is not archaeology. Unwillingness to take up old works, to modernize and streamline them for fresh production, betrays indifference, not praiseworthy caution. The Theater *welcomes* such modernization and has profited by it throughout those ages when it was most alive.

The original text remains intact for anyone who may want to reread it at home, for his own edification; those who want to be entertained by it will go to the

Theater, where it will be put on for them rid of those portions that have lost their freshness, brought up to date where its language is outworn, readapted to the taste of today.

Why is this legitimate?

Because in the Theater a work of art is no longer the work of the writer (which, after all, can always be preserved in some other way), but an act of life, realized on the stage from one moment to the next, with the cooperation of an audience that must find satisfaction in it.

If this were realized, we would have tangible proof of all I have said.

And I seem to have said what matters most. At this point it would be a simple task for me to indicate what approach to follow in building up — after Goldoni, down to our own time — the living repertory of the Italian Theater; but I don't think it would serve any purpose to spend further energy illustrating my premise with additional arguments — reaffirming, in other words, that even when this Theater of ours came under the influence of the foreign Theater, and especially the French, our productions yet stand out, in contrast with those others, in their greater realism and their greater fidelity to life; that there emerged, as in the *Commedia dell'arte*, regional characters and forms of expression — Milan or Venice, Piedmont or Naples or Sicily — by means of which our theatrical productions too, move in the great current of that constant reaction against intellectualism that is, after all, one of the greatest contributions of our genius to civilization; that, finally, after the long quest of the last century, the movement of our new Theater led happily and suddenly to the discovery of a virgin field, particularly suited to our dramatic talent, and found a true voice for the expression of new conflicts, abandoning all psychological study or indulgence, all normative aims, in order to realize without further ado the direct and free expression of those genuine emotions that are present and striving in the soul of every man, without fear of the contradictions that prevail in the emotional life, in the imagination, and in the will — contradictions that, until then, had been scrupulously avoided as incapable of being assimilated within the moral and esthetic integrity of the character. Out of this came, indirectly, the most caustic criticism of contemporary society ever articulated by writers of any age. It was nothing less than an illumination of the psychological state of man in our time; and it was recognized at once as characteristic and true, not only of the Italian soul, but also of our universal culture, in all those countries of the world that share in it. This explains the expansive force of the new Italian Theater, which has brought substance and spirit back into the work of so many European and American dramatists, directing their art to that vast virgin world of the unexplored life of human personality; something for which the creative artists of our time evidently must have felt a pressing need, since with the first suggestion provided by our creative original Italians, those others — almost to a man — have turned to confront that world with the most varied means and from the most diverse spiritual points of view.